"Stephen Barkley demonstrates the continuity between Old Testament prophecy and the practice of prophecy in contemporary charismatic churches. He builds the case for this correlation on careful examination of Old Testament prophetic passages and phenomenological and qualitative investigation and analysis of the contemporary practice of charismatic prophecy. Barkley makes a significant contribution to the theological understanding of biblical prophetic practice and its ongoing place in the contemporary church."

—**Steven M. Studebaker**, professor of systematic and historical theology,
McMaster Divinity College

Pentecostal Prophets

Pentecostal Prophets

Experience in Old Testament Perspective

Stephen D. Barkley

WIPF & STOCK · Eugene, Oregon

PENTECOSTAL PROPHETS
Experience in Old Testament Perspective

Wipf & Stock
An Imprint of Wipf and Stock Publishers
199 W. 8th Ave., Suite 3
Eugene, OR 97401

www.wipfandstock.com

PAPERBACK ISBN: 978-1-6667-6802-2
HARDCOVER ISBN: 978-1-6667-6803-9
EBOOK ISBN: 978-1-6667-6804-6

04/18/23

To my wife, Donna—who was an endless source of loving
encouragement, freeing up my time to research and write
(thank you for the noise-cancelling headphones);

to my boys, Ryan and Chase—who never fail to make me smile
and who enrich my life in more ways than I know;

and to my parents, David and Wendy—who raised me
in the Pentecostal tradition and were never hesitant
to express their pride in my accomplishments.

Contents

Tables

Preface

THIS BOOK BEGAN IN the fall of 2016. After almost twenty years of pastoral ministry in varies capacities—worship pastor, associate pastor, lead pastor—I felt the desire to return to school. I was accepted into McMaster Divinity College's Doctor of Practical Theology program and began to sort out my research topic. I knew that I wanted to study prophecy. I had recently read Abraham Heschel's *The Prophets* and was gripped by how his compelling prose about Amos, Isaiah, and Jeremiah resonated with how I had experienced the prophetic inspiration of God. On the other hand, I was deeply cynical. I had witnessed enough abuses of the gift of prophecy to want to write it all off—but I was Pentecostal! Acts 2, the Spirit-birthed prophethood of all believers, was my story.

Eventually, I narrowed down the focus of my study to one specific question: *How does the practice of charismatic prophecy in the Pentecostal Assemblies of Canada and Pentecostal Assemblies of Newfoundland and Labrador cohere with the experience of the Old Testament prophets?* One phenomenological study and some significant theological reflection later, I answered that question and defended it with a dissertation entitled "Charismatic Prophecy in the Pentecostal Assemblies of Canada: An Old Testament Perspective."

This book is essentially the published version of that dissertation with a few minor adjustments for clarity. As a dissertation, it follows traditional conventions like a methodology chapter and a literature review. If you're an academic, you'll understand. If you're a pastor reading this, feel free to skip over chapter 1. If you're someone who prophesies and are reading this for edification, you may want to begin with chapter 4, where I describe how prophets experience the inspiration of God before revisiting Jeremiah's experience in chapter 3.

In the end, I hope this book will inspire people to recognize and value the gift of prophecy. Yes, there are abuses of this gift, both intentional and unintentional. Despite this, there's something beautiful and upbuilding when people gain the courage to humbly share what God reveals to them. They practice their birthright as heirs to the Old Testament prophets and ultimately Jesus, prophet *par excellence*, whose Spirit still inspires the lips of his followers today.

Acknowledgments

The practice of prophecy is, by its nature, a communal event. I am fortunate to have been involved in a variety of settings where this gift was encouraged. I grew up hearing words of prophecy uttered—often in Sunday night services—at Bancroft Pentecostal Tabernacle. I am indebted to the saints there whose faithfulness to speak God's word sparked my sense of wonder at this mysterious practice. Professionally, I have served three congregations in a pastoral capacity: Faith Alive Christian Centre in Mississauga, New Life Assembly in Petrolia, and Wellington Street Pentecostal Church in Bracebridge. I am especially indebted to my congregation in Bracebridge, who served as the immediate setting of this project.

A variety of pastoral leaders have also inspired me. I am grateful for Terry Burns and Tim Brown for the many discussions we had about prophecy during our time together in Petrolia. Despite the challenge of cynicism, we all recognized something real and valuable at the core of this practice.

I have made friends with my DPT colleagues throughout this process. Thank you, David Long, for the many conversations we shared as we commuted to and from Hamilton together (even if the conversations were so engaging that we regularly missed our exit)! Thanks also to Merv Budd, Heather Card, and Greg Reader for the encouragement (and group-therapy) required for this project to reach the finish line.

Finally, I offer my deepest thanks to my doctoral advisor, Dr. Paul Evans; second reader, Dr. Steven Studebaker; and external examiner, Dr. Jacqueline Grey. Their guidance and insight have improved every page of this project.

S.D.G.

Abbreviations

ABD   *The Anchor Bible Dictionary*. 6 vols. Edited by David Noel Freedman. New York: Doubleday, 1992.

AG   Assemblies of God

CP   Charismatic Prophecy

DOP   *Dictionary of the Old Testament Prophets*. Edited by Mark J. Boda and J. Gordon McConville. Downers Grove: IVP Academic, 2012.

NIDPCM   *The New International Dictionary of Pentecostal Charismatic Movements*. Revised and expanded edition. Edited by Stanley M. Burgess and Eduard M. van der Maas. Grand Rapids: Zondervan, 2002.

PAOC   Pentecostal Assemblies of Canada

PAONL   Pentecostal Assemblies of Newfoundland and Labrador

PLR   Practice-Led Research

Introduction

THE CHURCH WAS UNSETTLED—FOR good reason. Our small community had just suffered a homicide in the driveway across from the church during a youth event. The congregation felt uncomfortable, confused, disconnected. As I transitioned the church from the song service to the sermon, I paused to bring the congregation before God in prayer. Out of the silence that followed the final song, I prayed for the families of the victims—that they would be comforted and know the peace of God. I prayed that God would give us the ability to be agents of his light in the midst of darkness.

With my final "amen" still reverberating in the room, Sheila spoke.[1] In a confident, passionate tone she declared the sovereignty of God over and above the chaos. Sheila, a senior in our congregation, has been a faithful Christian her entire life. Her message chained Scripture together from throughout the canon into a fluid prophetic statement of God's final victory over everything that threatens his good creation. Speaking with Sheila a few days later, she confided how she felt nervous about speaking out. She had only been a member of our congregation for a year and had never prophesied here before. Furthermore, this form of charismatic utterance is rare in our reserved congregation. Despite these misgivings, Sheila said, "I had to speak. I could hardly wait until your prayer was done, pastor, before I just had to let it all out!" As she explained this to me, I considered how Jeremiah perceived God's unspoken word as "something like a burning fire shut up in [his] bones" (Jer 20:9).[2]

Sheila's message had the immediate effect of settling the disquiet of the congregation. We paused to reflect and thank God for his message—on Pentecost Sunday of all days. The prophecy snapped the people's attention from surrounding tragedy to the sovereign God. Following the

---

1. Throughout this book, all names have been changed and personal data has been confused to protect anonymity.

2. All Scripture unless otherwise noted is cited from the NRSV.

service, people thanked Sheila for being faithful to share the message she had received. In casual discussions with members of the congregation in the days that followed I heard expressions like, "Isn't it wonderful" and "That was *so* good."

Looking back on this situation, several questions come to mind. From an academic perspective, I wonder if Sheila faithfully exegeted the multitude of Scripture references woven into her prophecy. Should sound exegesis even be required of modern-day prophets?[3] What is the relationship between prophets and the biblical canon, both the Old and New Testaments? As the leader of the worship service, the question of discernment is also front-of-mind. Any pastor who has led a charismatic worship service that includes prophecy knows the fearsome responsibility of evaluating whether the message is appropriate for the congregation. Is the pastor solely responsible to discern the validity of the prophetic word or should that burden be shared with the prophet—or even the congregation? I also marvel at the emotional weight of Sheila's message. Her voice quivered with a sense of authority and awe as she *declared* what she had heard from God. In that moment, Sheila reminded me of the Old Testament prophets—fiery people who spoke with authority. Sheila's emotional response to the prophetic impulse was echoed by the congregation, including this pastor! Some people began to weep while others sat down as their knees felt weak. I wonder what elicited this emotional and physical response. Could this be explained exclusively using the social sciences or is there something uniquely numinous about the situation?[4] Questions like these regarding the experience of the prophets sparked my desire to examine prophecy and modern-day prophets more closely. In particular, is there a connection between the Old Testament prophets and the prophets of today? Out of these questions, a specific research question was formulated that would guide this study: *How does the practice of charismatic prophecy (CP) in the Pentecostal Assemblies of Canada (PAOC) and Pentecostal Assemblies of Newfoundland and Labrador (PAONL) cohere with the experience of the Old Testament prophets?*

---

3. I use the word "prophets" for simplicity here and throughout this book to refer to people who practice the gift of prophecy. I do not intend to posit a theoretical distinction between the office and the gift of prophecy, a distinction that will be explored in chapter 2.

4. Poloma uses anthropological and sociological perspectives to account for the experience of the divine in *Main Street Mystics*, an account of the Toronto Blessing. See especially her use of Turner's "floating world," a way to describe that liminal space wherein people encounter the numinous (68–81).

Prophecy in Pentecostalism

CP has been a significant emphasis of Pentecostalism from its earliest days until the present. At the Topeka Revival, a number of Charles Parham's Bible school students "received the Holy Ghost, *and prophesied*, and cloven tongues could be seen upon their heads."[5] Here, prophecy is closely linked with the reception of the Spirit. For the early Pentecostals, their understanding of Scripture followed a "revivalistic-restorationist" interpretation.[6] Their experience of Spirit baptism with the sign of speaking in tongues formed an experiential presupposition and subsequent verification that enabled them to understand the Acts narrative in a new light.[7] A consequence of this is their understanding of prophecy. If the Bible said that prophecy follows Spirit baptism, early Pentecostals expected to experience this phenomenon. This connection between Spirit baptism and prophecy continued at Azusa Street. In the first issue of the *Apostolic Faith*, both Acts 2:17–18 as well as Acts 19:6 were cited as sources for the correlation of Spirit baptism with prophecy.[8] This link can be demonstrated even more strongly. In one of the columns from the first *Apostolic Faith*, the author teaches about Cornelius receiving the Spirit in Acts 10, claiming, "The Holy Ghost fell on them as at the beginning and they spoke with tongues and prophesied."[9] Technically, prophecy is not mentioned in the Acts 10 account. However, the experience of receiving the Spirit and prophesying had become so normative that it was assumed. At Azusa Street, preaching was a response to the spontaneous leading of the Spirit and was identified with prophecy.[10] Josh P. S. Samuel

5. Seymour, *Azusa Papers*, 6, emphasis added. For the roots of American Pentecostalism, see Hollenweger, *Pentecostals*, 19–28. There is vigorous debate in Pentecostal circles regarding the origin of the movement. Scholars including Yong eschew the traditional America-centric origin account for a more global explanation (Yong, "Science, Sighs, and Signs," 192). Whether or not Pentecostalism began in America, everyone agrees that the Azusa Street revival is of central significance.

6. Archer, *Pentecostal Hermeneutic*, 102. The "Bible Reading Method" of interpretation used by the early Pentecostals was similar to methods employed by contemporary holiness movements (99). Archer describes this method of interpretation more fully as a "'pre-critical,' canonical and text centered synchronic approach from a revivalistic-restorationist biblicist perspective" (102).

7. Stronstad explores the function of Spirit Baptism as a hermeneutical key in the third chapter of *Spirit, Scripture, and Theology*, 39–59.

8. Seymour, *Azusa Papers*, 9.

9. Seymour, *Azusa Papers*, 16.

10. Samuel describes how preaching was a response to the perceived immediacy of the Spirit (*Holy Spirit in Worship Music*, 39).

writes: "Sermon manuscripts were unnecessary, since preachers should rely on the spontaneous leading of the Spirit."[11]

The Pentecostal movement appeared in Canada quickly, with revivals igniting in Toronto in late 1906 and Winnipeg in 1907.[12] The pattern experienced at Topeka, Kansas, and Azusa Street, California, continued. People received the Spirit with the gift of speaking in tongues. Again, prophecy was central to the Pentecostal experience. The first issue of *The Promise*, the first Pentecostal magazine from Canada, records the prophetic interpretation of a woman who spoke in tongues. The issue ends with a poem "given in the language, to Mrs. Hebden and also interpreted."[13] Canadian historian Thomas William Miller cited personal correspondence from Effie Moyer (née Brewer) to her sister Mamie McPherson in 1911 that vividly recounts the connection between Spirit baptism and prophecy.

> I fell under the Power of God and I commenced to shake. I had always been opposed to the shaking . . . I soon commenced to speak in an unknown Tongue . . . The next evening . . . the Power came over me and I commenced to give messages to the cold, careless church members, also some of the unsaved. *God spoke through me* for about one hour like that, telling the people Jesus was coming soon . . . Oh Mamie, it was more real than my own life. *God . . . wanted me to give the same message to you.*[14]

While the word prophecy is not explicitly mentioned in Moyer's testimony, it is clear that a consequence of experiencing "the Power" was that God now *spoke through* the recipient—another way of describing prophecy. Canadian Pentecostals along with other global expressions have long valued "the connection between Spirit and prophecy."[15]

As the first generation of Pentecostals gave way to the next, a new revival took place in North Battleford, Saskatchewan, in 1948, known as "The New Order of the Latter Rain."[16] This was an "inherently Canadian Pentecostal

11. Samuel, *Holy Spirit in Worship Music*, 46.

12. Miller, *Canadian Pentecostals*, 39. It should be remembered that Pentecostalism is a transnational movement. Wilkinson and Althouse argue that Pentecostalism "is characterized by a series of global flows or movements of the Spirit which travel freely across borders" ("Winds of the Spirit," 3).

13. Mittelstadt and Courtney, "Canadian Pentecostal Reader," 17–18. The "language" referred to here is *glossolalia*, or speaking in tongues.

14. Miller, *Canadian Pentecostals*, 48, emphasis added.

15. Wilkinson and Althouse, "Like a Mighty Rushing Wind," 4.

16. Faupel, "New Order," 240.

innovation" that impacted Pentecostal understanding around the world.[17] Those who identified with the Latter Rain movement understood themselves to be experiencing the "new thing" Isaiah prophesied (43:19). Richard M. Riss writes: "The movement was characterized by many reports of healings and other miraculous phenomena."[18] Most important for this study is their renewed emphasis on the significance of prophecy. Armed with Eph 4:11, they understood that their revival would restore the "Ascension Gift Ministries" including the missing offices of apostle and prophet.[19] While apostles were the first gift in the list, prophets were a close second, "proclaiming the 'mysteries of God' [and] making them plain to the church."[20] The Latter Rain movement described three levels of prophets.

> First, there were those who had "the gift of prophecy" that functioned in the local church. Second, there were prophets who, like the apostles, were given authority to minister to the church at large. Finally, there were "a few prophets . . . whose ministry will be in the extraordinary use of the term. These are 'raised-up' for special purposes. They shall enter a phase of ministry such as Samuel, Elijah, Moses, and Ezekiel. There will be unusual manifestations of 'the word of knowledge' and the 'word of wisdom' in their ministry."[21]

While not all Pentecostals would agree with the three levels of prophecy described by the Latter Rain movement, the movement does illustrate the high value placed on prophecy by second-generation Canadian Pentecostals.[22]

The connection between Pentecostalism and prophecy has been carried into the present in various forms of Pentecostalism, including the

---

17. Wilkinson and Althouse, "Like a Mighty Rushing Wind," 11.

18. Riss, "Latter Rain Movement," 830.

19. These gifts, or offices, are named "Ascension Gift Ministries" on the basis of Eph 4:8–11: "When he ascended up on high, he led captivity captive and gave gifts unto men . . . And he gave some apostles; and some, prophets; and some, evangelists; and some, pastors and teachers" (KJV).

20. Faupel, "New Order," 249.

21. Faupel, "New Order," 249–50.

22. The PAOC today prefers to view prophecy as a gift rather than an office. "In the Old Testament, for the most part, God chose and called selected individuals to function in the *office* of a prophet (Jeremiah 1:4, 5). Under the new covenant, while all Spirit-filled believers share the actual presence of the Holy Spirit and thus have access to all of His gifts including prophecy, there are also those in the body that operate regularly and consistently in this gift" (PAOC, "Contemporary Prophets," 5).

Third Wave or Charismatic movement.[23] With roots in the Latter Rain movement, the Charismatic movement also highlighted the restoration of the fivefold ministry of Ephesians with an emphasis on apostles and prophets. Catch the Fire, the current name of the church that was at the heart of the Toronto Blessing in the 1990s, is an example of a modern-day charismatic community that highly values prophecy.[24] In particular, their practice known as "soaking prayer" facilitates the use of prophetic gifts. In soaking prayer, people attend a service where lights are turned low and candles are sometimes lit. People bring pillows and blankets with them, find a place on the floor, and "soak" in the presence of God as calming worship music is played, either by live musicians or recorded audio.[25] One of the regional directors of this charismatic practice made the following observation.

> One of the things that the renewal has done is to activate and encourage the prophetic gifts with people. We've been encouraged to "look" to see what the Lord will show or say. And I can personally say that I have learned to use this gift on a regular basis. I believe that it is the fulfillment of Joel, Chapter 2, and quoted in Acts 2, that says I will pour out My Spirit on all flesh, and your sons and your daughters will prophesy . . . So in renewal, when the Holy Spirit is pouring out in a tangible way, it seems natural that there would be more prophecy, and words of wisdom, words of knowledge, etc.[26]

It should be noted that the phrases used by that regional director are almost verbatim those used by William Seymour in the *Apostolic Faith* over a century earlier.[27] To receive the Spirit naturally leads to prophecy.

Classical Pentecostals still emphasize the importance of prophecy in local church praxis. In a 2001 position paper, the Assemblies of God (AG) argued that

---

23. Some Pentecostals refer to the movement using the metaphor of waves. The first wave began with Azusa Street and includes Classical Pentecostals, including the PAOC. The second wave refers to the Charismatic Renewal that occurred within historic mainline denominations in the 1960s and 70s. The third wave refers to independent charismatics, including groups like the Kansas City Prophets and the Toronto Blessing. Of course, there is much cross-pollination between Pentecostal denominations and fellowships today, regardless of their origins. See Wilkinson and Althouse, *Catch the Fire*, 23–27, for a concise overview of the origins of charismatic Christianity.

24. For a description of the Toronto Blessing, see Barkley, "Toronto Blessing."

25. Wilkinson and Althouse, *Catch the Fire*, 102.

26. Wilkinson and Althouse, *Catch the Fire*, 119.

27. Seymour, *Azusa Papers*, 6.

> while it is too much to say every utterance of a believer is a
> prophecy, nonetheless, the theme of Acts is that every believer
> receives the power of the Holy Spirit to be a prophetic witness
> to the risen Lord Jesus Christ . . . All believers are inducted into
> a universal "prophethood" and are endowed with one or more
> spiritual gifts, many of which have directly to do with wise, in-
> structive, and edifying utterances.[28]

Here the concept of prophecy is expanded from a specific utterance to a general disposition that encompasses various Pauline gifts, including teaching, wisdom, knowledge, and tongues. North of the border, the PAOC also emphasizes this universal prophethood of all believers, stressing the need for prophecy to strengthen, encourage, and comfort believers while at the same time convincing unbelievers of the presence of God. The gift of prophecy "functions alongside other ministry gifts in the work of equipping believers with unity, Christlike character, doctrinal stability and balanced gift-based functionality, preparing them for effective ministry as the living embodiment of Christ in this world."[29] Later in this book I will interact with global research from Mark J. Cartledge (England), Samuel Muindi (Kenya), Dennis Lum (Singapore), and Tanya Harris (Australia) that confirms and nuances the main point of this section: from the earliest days until the present, Pentecostals are inextricably linked with prophecy.[30]

Defining Prophecy

This book will explore the level of coherence between the experience of Old Testament prophets and modern-day charismatic prophets.[31] To do this, a working definition of how prophecy is understood in Pentecostal churches is required. This definition will proceed in three steps. First, the broader Lucan category of the prophethood of all believers will be examined. This step will include consideration of the Old Testament roots of the prophetic

---

28. AG, "Apostles and Prophets," 9.

29. PAOC, "Contemporary Prophets," 6.

30. See Cartledge, "Charismatic Prophecy," "Charismatic Prophecy: A Definition," "Charismatic Prophecy and New Testament Prophecy," *Narratives and Numbers*, and *Practical Theology*; Muindi, "Nature and Significance" and *Pentecostal-Charismatic Prophecy*; Lum, *Practice of Prophecy*; and Harris, "Where Pentecostalism and Evangelicalism Part Ways" (parts 1 and 2). Harris's PhD dissertation, "Hearing God's Voice," was released following the completion of this study.

31. The methodology used to accomplish this task is the subject of chapter 1.

experience. Next, the Pauline gift of prophecy will be explored. Finally, with a biblical understanding in place, a definition of CP will be developed.

The Prophethood of All Believers

The AG and PAOC position papers cited above both refer to the prophethood of all believers—a theme that forms the context wherein the gift of prophecy is practiced. The scholar who expounded this theme most fully is Canadian Pentecostal Roger Stronstad in his study entitled *The Prophethood of All Believers*.[32] Prophecy in the Old Testament begins with Abraham, who was identified as a prophet by Abimelek, king of Gerar (Gen 20:7), and ends with the final writing prophet, Malachi. However, it is Moses who holds the paradigmatic role as *the* prophet who launched the prophetic movement in Israel. Moses fulfilled the prophet's core task: to hear from God and to pass that word on to others.[33] In Deuteronomy, set near the end of Moses' life, Moses prophesied: "The LORD your God will raise up for you a prophet like me from among your own people; you shall heed such a prophet" (Deut 18:15). Moses was succeeded by Joshua, and although Moses laid hands on him and he was filled with the Spirit of wisdom (Deut 34:9), he did not prove to be the prophet Moses spoke of. In the final words of the Torah it was confessed that "never since has there arisen a prophet in Israel like Moses, whom the LORD knew face to face. He was unequaled for all the signs and wonders that the LORD sent him to perform in the land of Egypt . . . and for all the mighty deeds and all the terrifying displays of power that Moses performed in the sight of all Israel" (Deut 34:10–12). It was another Joshua—Jesus—who would fulfill that role.[34]

Luke made it clear that Jesus is the eschatological anointed prophet who summed up no less than five Old Testament prophetic traditions. He is "the prophet like Isaiah, the prophet like Elijah and Elisha, like the rejected prophets, the royal prophet, and the prophet like Moses."[35] Since Moses is the paradigmatic prophetic figure in the Old Testament, it is important

---

32. In addition to this work, Stronstad also touches on this theme in his earlier *Charismatic Theology of St. Luke* and in a new chapter added to the second edition of his *Spirit, Scripture, and Theology* entitled, "The Rebirth of Prophecy" (159–91).

33. This brief description of prophecy will be fleshed out fully in the following section.

34. Jesus' name in Hebrew is transliterated *Yeshua* and is anglicized as Joshua.

35. Stronstad, *Prophethood*, 112.

to consider how Jesus was a prophet like Moses.[36] In at least one rabbinic tradition, prophecy ceased in Israel with Haggai, Zechariah, and Malachi.[37] Luke began his Gospel with a burst of prophetic activity from Zechariah, Mary, Simeon, and Anna. This sets the stage for Jesus. Luke presents Jesus' prophetic ministry in two phases: in Galilee (3:1—9:50) and on the road (Luke 9:51—Acts 1:11). Each phase begins and ends with a theophany that confirms Jesus' prophetic ministry: the presence of God at his baptism, the transfiguration, and Jesus' ascension. The imagery of the transfiguration is particularly noteworthy (Luke 9:28–36) since it is here that God directly confirms that Jesus is the prophet like Moses.

> There on the so-called Mount of Transfiguration Jesus' metamorphosis (a.k.a., transfiguration) matches Moses' earlier glorification on Mount Sinai; his impending departure (i.e., ἔξοδος) matches Israel's earlier Exodus from Egypt; the theophanic cloud of God's presence, which envelopes Jesus and his companions, matches the cloud of God's presence which earlier had enveloped Mount Sinai. Finally, God's command to "listen to Him" fulfills Moses' command to Israel that they must listen to the prophet like himself whom God would raise up to be his successor.[38]

Stronstad's case for Jesus as the fulfillment of Moses' prophecy is more broadly based than the transfiguration alone, but on Mount Tabor the major prophetic themes come to a head.

Luke continues his prophet-like-Moses theme on the Day of Pentecost. By exploring the septuagintal language of Luke-Acts, Stronstad sees a classic transfer motif in Acts 2. When Moses transferred leadership authority to the seventy elders, "[the] LORD came down in the cloud and spoke to [Moses], and took some of the spirit that was on him and put it on the seventy elders; and when the spirit rested upon them, *they prophesied*" (Num 11:25, emphasis added). In a similar way, Acts 2 records the transfer of the Spirit from Jesus, the "Spirit-anointed, Spirit-ful, Spirit-led, and Spirit-empowered eschatological prophet"[39] to his prophetic community. "Just as the descent of the Spirit upon Jesus makes him the Spirit anointed prophet, so the pouring out of the Spirit upon the disciples makes them

---

36. Stronstad, *Spirit, Scripture, and Theology*, 162.

37. Stronstad cites *t. Sotah* 8:2 (*Spirit, Scripture, and Theology*, 163). This claim will be assessed in chapter 2.

38. Stronstad, *Spirit, Scripture, and Theology*, 167.

39. Stronstad, *Prophethood*, 6.

the prophethood of all believers."[40] In the old covenant, God created his people to be a nation of priests (Exod 19:5, 6). In the new covenant, God transforms his people into a nation, a community, of prophets.

It is within this milieu—the prophetic community—that Pentecostals practice prophecy. It is understood that although God may gift people differently at different times, those who have received the Spirit of God are empowered for prophetic speech. The prophethood of all believers is the setting where the gift of prophecy is practiced.

Gift of Prophecy

Shifting focus from the prophethood of all believers to the gift of prophecy takes us from Lukan to Pauline literature. In doing so, it is critical to avoid importing Lukan thought into Pauline language and vice versa. Paul must be interpreted on his own terms. "Paul's written doctrine of the Holy Spirit is much more complex than the doctrines of the Spirit which are to be found in either Luke's writings or John's writings."[41] While Luke and Paul both emphasize the theme of Spirit-empowered service, Paul further adds the themes of salvation and sanctification.[42] Despite the additional complexity, Paul, along with Luke, recognize Jesus as the "fountainhead of prophecy, fulfilling that of which Moses is the original."[43] Where Luke stressed the prophethood of *all* believers, Paul describes how the gift of prophecy functions within the church. It is to this gift of prophecy that we now turn.

Paul lists spiritual gifts in three of his epistles: 1 Cor 12–14, Rom 12:6–8, and Eph 4:11.[44] Each of these lists contain unique as well as overlapping terms that suggests that these lists are not intended to be comprehensive but rather contextual.[45] The gifts can be generally organized under three

---

40. Stronstad, *Prophethood*, 113.

41. Stronstad, *Spirit, Scripture, and Theology*, 183.

42. Stronstad, *Spirit, Scripture, and Theology*, 156–57. Menzies argues that Paul was the first Christian to "attribute soteriological functions to the Spirit," and that Luke followed the intertestamental understanding of the Spirit as the source of prophecy (*Development of Early Christian Pneumatology*, 48).

43. Stronstad, *Spirit, Scripture, and Theology*, 183.

44. I use the common term "spiritual gift" as a way of including the various New Testament expressions, including "'spiritual things' (Gk. *pneumatika*), 'graces' or 'favors' (*charismata*), and 'showings' or 'manifestations' (*phanerōseis*)," as well as "'workings' (*energēmata*) and 'ministries' (*diakoniai*)" (Michaels, "Gifts of the Spirit," 665).

45. Fee acknowledges the difficulty in organizing these lists due to the "ad hoc" nature

headings: Spirit manifestations within the worshipping community (e.g., glossolalia and prophecy), deeds of service (e.g., serving and giving), and specific ministries (e.g., apostles and teachers).[46] The gift of prophecy takes pride of place within the manifestation gifts. Statistically, this gift is mentioned more than any others, "implying the widest range of occurrence in the Pauline churches."[47] This is unsurprising given the value that Paul places on this gift. "Pursue love and strive for the spiritual gifts, and *especially that you may prophesy*" (1 Cor 14:1, emphasis added). The details of this gift will be examined in the literature review (chapter 2). For now, it is enough to recognize that the practice of CP is generally understood as a manifestation of the gift of prophecy that is situated contextually within the prophetic community created when the Holy Spirit was transferred from Jesus, *the paradigmatic eschatological prophet*, to his followers.

Charismatic Prophecy

With the prophethood of all believers now established, within which people practice the Pauline gift of prophecy, it is possible to define the practice of modern-day CP. Prophecy is "a *Leitmotiv*, both in Scripture and in the church."[48] Understandings of this practice are correspondingly broad. In modern society, the term covers everything from secular social commentary[49] to the directive prophetic practice of the Apostolic Church.[50] C. M. Robeck Jr. describes three ways prophecy is understood in the church. It is either "(1) an oracle, spontaneously inspired by the Holy Spirit and spoken in a specific situation; (2) a form of expositional preaching from the biblical text; or (3) a public pronouncement of a moral or ethical nature that confronts society."[51] The idea of prophecy as a "predictive word of future events" is rooted in the practice of various cultures in the ancient Near East

---

of Paul's letters and the "ambiguity" of the lists. He concludes that the gifts must be first understood within their context (Fee, "Gifts of the Spirit," 342).

46. Fee, "Gifts of the Spirit," 345.

47. Fee, "Gifts of the Spirit," 346.

48. Muindi, "Nature and Significance," 1.

49. Roberts, "Jon Stewart."

50. Thomas, "Teaching and Practice." Directive prophecy refers to the experience of relying on prophetic messages to give specific direction to current actions such as purchasing a house, marrying a spouse, or committing to a mission trip.

51. Robeck, "Prophecy," 999.

and has been emphasized in fundamentalist circles.[52] In order to study the phenomenon of CP, a more precise definition is required.

I will draw on three definitions that build upon each other to provide a basic understanding of the practice. Max Turner defines CP as "oracular speech; the rendering of a message considered by a Christian to have been imparted to him [or her] directly by the Spirit in a 'word' or vision."[53] This revelation contains "particularistic knowledge—not merely general principles that could be deduced, for example, by illuminated reading of the Torah, or from the Gospel Tradition, or from apostolic didache."[54] This definition includes three key elements. First, a revelatory impulse is at the root of the practice. That is, the prophet is not simply a clever person, but one who believes they are receiving something from God. Second, the impulse leads to oracular speech. That is, the prophet speaks that which was revealed by God. Third, the content of the revelation contains particularistic knowledge. Turner's definition is a good place to start. Muindi and Cartledge expand the definition based on their empirical research.

For Muindi, "Charismatic prophecy is an invasive oracular utterance inspired by a perceived immediacy of divine presence, or the Holy Spirit, which, perceptually, impacted the human deep unconscious dimension with revelatory impulses."[55] Muindi keeps Turner's oracular speech/utterance while dropping his claim for particularistic knowledge. Muindi clarifies Turner's phrase—revelatory impulse—in three ways. First, Muindi uses the powerful term *invasive*. The revelatory impulse is something from outside that intrudes on the prophet. Second, this invasion is perceived as an *immediacy of the divine presence*. The prophets speak when they recognize the presence of God. Third, the Holy Spirit communicates to prophets by impacting their *deep unconscious dimension*. This is a more difficult clarification to understand since one cannot speak unconsciously and consciously simultaneously. Cartledge sheds light on this unconscious dimension in his work on the Toronto Blessing by using Patrick Dixon's altered state of consciousness lens. An altered state of consciousness is "that state between our normal waking state and our unconscious sleeping state. It is the state of the daydream or the vision."[56] These are complex states that

52. Robeck, "Prophecy," 999.

53. Turner, "Spiritual Gifts," 46.

54. Turner, "Spiritual Gifts," 12.

55. Muindi, "Nature and Significance," 255.

56. Cartledge, *Practical Theology*, 181.

"have been used by the Holy Spirit as a means by which revelation has been imparted."[57] These visionary states are common in Scripture. For example, God reconfirmed his covenant with Abram as the sun was going down and Abram was placed into a deep sleep (Gen 15:12). Daniel Tappeiner draws a connection between the "revelatory state of mind" and the hypnagogic state: "that particular state of consciousness experienced by an individual which precedes and leads to another state called sleep."[58] While there is no consensus, there are phenomenological descriptions and biblical examples for understanding the communication of the divine impulse to the human deep unconscious dimension.

Mark Cartledge provides the fullest definition of CP:

> In the charismatic movement the term "prophecy" is used in a technical sense to refer to a message from God to someone (an individual, group, local community, nation or society) by means of a spokesperson. This usually occurs through the medium of a revelatory experience—that is, an experience such as a vision, dream, mental picture, words coming to mind, or other such experiences, through which the person believes that God is communicating directly.[59]

For Cartledge, the message is transferred *from* God *through* a spokesperson *to* a recipient. The recipient of a prophetic message can be as unique as a person or as broad as a nation. Cartledge expands Turner and Muindi's revelatory impulse. God can speak to the prophet through a variety of experiences, including pictures, words, inspired prayer, the interpretation of tongues, dreams and visions, audible voice, reception of knowledge, Scripture verses coming to mind, physical sensation, subjective impressions, and compulsion to speak or write something down. In this diverse list, Cartledge has accounted for all the data in its rich diversity, illuminating the multiplex nature of CP.[60]

I follow Cartledge's empirical research in understanding CP in broad terms. Biblically speaking, CP includes the Pauline gifts of prophecy, word of

---

57. Cartledge, *Practical Theology*, 190.

58. Tappeiner, "Psychological Paradigm," 27.

59. Cartledge, "Charismatic Prophecy and New Testament Prophecy," 17.

60. Cartledge, "Charismatic Prophecy," 79–82. From a practical theological perspective, this list demonstrates how situations are "complex, multifaceted entities which need to be examined with care, rigour and discernment if they are to be effectively understood" (Swinton and Mowat, *Practical Theology*, 15).

wisdom, word of knowledge, and tongues (*glossolalia*) and interpretation.[61] Interpreting *glossolalia* as prophecy is challenging since it is practiced in two overlapping ways. In the first place, *glossolalia* can be a prayerful expression of worship toward God. In this sense, it is not a prophetic act. Although it is a revelatory experience, the goal is not to convey "a message from God to someone . . . by means of a spokesperson,"[62] but to convey a message from the worshiper to God. In the second place, *glossolalia* can become prophecy when it is intended as a message from God to the congregation. When the spiritual gift of interpretation follows the *glossolalia*, its prophetic intent is actualized. The distinction between these two forms of *glossolalia*, however, is fuzzy. Both are revelatory experiences. On some occasions a *glossolalic* speech-act is spoken in a declarative mode but no interpretation follows. In this case I will interpret the message as part of the broader phenomenon of prophecy. Samuel Muindi notes that the significance of CP goes "beyond what may be deciphered from an exegetical analysis of the linguistic content of the prophecy utterance."[63] The impact of the prophetic speech-act transcends grammar and "has far reaching . . . effects on individual and congregational lives."[64] This justifies the inclusion of uninterpreted *glossolalia* as a part of the prophetic phenomenon.

Research Question

With the significance of prophecy in the Pentecostal tradition emphasized and the nature of prophecy defined, we can now return to the research question at the centre of this book. The PAOC defines a prophet simply as "one who has heard directly from the Lord and who speaks on His behalf."[65] This holds true whether the prophet is Jeremiah, Simeon, or one of the billions of global believers—those of the prophethood of all believers. The research question seeks to tie the modern practice of CP to its Old Testament roots by asking: *How does the practice of CP in the PAOC and PAONL cohere with the experience of the Old Testament prophets?* In saying this, I am suggesting the practice does indeed cohere, although this coherence is not always valued. The PAOC's official position paper on

61. Cartledge, "Charismatic Prophecy: A Definition," 88–95.

62. Cartledge, "Charismatic Prophecy and New Testament Prophecy," 17.

63. Muindi, "Nature and Significance," 243.

64. Muindi, "Nature and Significance," 243.

65. PAOC, "Contemporary Prophets," 2.

"Contemporary Prophets and Prophecy" is careful to describe the differences between Old Testament prophets and charismatic prophets.[66] The position paper does not unpack the congruity between Old Testament and charismatic prophets with the same rigor. Since the purpose of the position paper arose from a need to address the issue of people claiming the office of prophet in local churches, it was more important to show how modern prophets were distinct from the Old Testament tradition.[67] This book will move in the other direction, seeking to highlight congruencies between the Old Testament and charismatic prophets.

The Significance of this Study

The contribution of this work to the theoretical and theological significance of CP is threefold. First, it will fill in a lacuna regarding the practice of CP in Canada. To date, four scholars have published practical empirical research work on CP, each in non-Canadian contexts (England, Kenya, Singapore, and Australia).[68] How closely their research reflects Canadian practice in the PAOC and PAONL remains to be seen. The phenomenological approach to qualitative research utilized in this study will provide valuable data to situate the Canadian practice of prophecy in global perspective.

Second, existing data on PAOC spirituality has provided an anomalous result. While no CP-specific work has been done in the Canadian context, research by Adam Stewart and Andrew Gabriel on PAOC spirituality has included CP as one of a number of Pentecostal practices. Stewart and Gabriel

---

66. This is the only official statement the PAOC has made on CP. As will be explained in chapter 2, the reason for describing the differences between Old Testament and charismatic prophets is at least in part to safeguard the unique authority of inspired Scripture. It is telling that the only mention of the word "prophet" in the PAOC's "Statement of Fundamental and Essential Truths" refers to the companion of the Beast of Revelation! The PAOC's revised "Statement of Essential Truths" does not mention prophecy by name, although it states that Spirit Baptism empowers people with "speech and action."

67. PAOC, "Contemporary Prophets," 1. As mentioned earlier, the issue of modern-day apostles and prophets arose from the *Latter Rain Movement* and impacts classical Pentecostalism through the influence of the Charismatic Movement.

68. E.g., Cartledge, "Charismatic Prophecy," "Charismatic Prophecy: A Definition," "Charismatic Prophecy and New Testament Prophecy," *Narratives and Numbers*, and *Practical Theology*; Muindi, "Nature and Significance," later published as *Pentecostal-Charismatic Prophecy*; Lum, *Practice of Prophecy*; and Harris, "Where Pentecostalism and Evangelicalism Part Ways" (parts 1 and 2). Harris's PhD dissertation, "Hearing God's Voice," was released following the completion of this study.

conducted a survey of PAOC credential holders in 2014 in order to compare and contrast current beliefs and practices with a similar study conducted in 1985/86 by Carl Verge.[69] They determined that "engagement in some spiritual practices traditionally associated with the gifts of the Spirit . . . experienced a decline in frequency."[70] CP resists this diminishing trend. Whereas in 1985/6, credential holders prophesied on average five times per year, that figure has now doubled.[71] This indicates a "departure from the overall narrative of decline in spiritual practices."[72] The reason for this increase in practice is uncertain. Stewart and Gabriel suggest the emphasis may have shifted from traditional manifestations such as *glossolalia* to "less emotive and intimate applications, such as prophecy."[73] This suggestion, however, presupposes that prophecy is a less emotive and intimate experience than other spiritual gifts. Muindi's sacramental-experiential model does not support this.[74] Another possibility is that Pentecostal clergy interpret the gift of prophecy more as inspired preaching than a deeply sacramental experience. It is clear there is work to be done to understand how Canadians practice CP. The phenomenological investigation recounted in chapter 4 will provide insight into the shifting nature of PAOC spirituality.

Third, Pentecostals have traditionally made limited use of the Classical Prophets. The prophets are regularly used for messianic predictions (e.g., Isa 7:14; 9:6–7; 53:4–5), for prophecies about the Spirit (e.g., Ezek 37:1–14) and even for eisegetic proof texts to encourage the faithful (e.g., Jer 29:11) and raise funds (e.g., Mal 3:8–10). The prophet Joel is a notable exception here, given the significance of his prophecy in Peter's interpretation of the Pentecost event (Acts 2:17–21; cf. Joel 2:28–32).[75] By exploring

69. The main presentation of this research can be found in *Pneuma: The Journal of the Society for Pentecostal Studies* as "Changes in Clergy Belief and Practice." The chief insights of this research were shared with participants of the study online as "Highlights of the 2014 Survey of PAOC Credential Holders." Finally, the work was presented on a more popular level in a series of three articles in *Enrich*, the PAOC's leadership journal: "Missional Vitality and the future of the PAOC," "Spiritual Vitality among PAOC Credential Holders," and "Theological Vitality in the PAOC Today."

70. Stewart and Gabriel, "Spiritual Vitality," 27.

71. Stewart and Gabriel, "Spiritual Vitality," 26, 28.

72. Stewart and Gabriel, "Spiritual Vitality," 28.

73. Stewart and Gabriel, "Spiritual Vitality," 28.

74. Muindi, *Charismatic Prophecy*, 191. This model will be explored in chapter 2.

75. McQueen argues that the tripartite structure of Joel—lament (1:1—2:17), salvation (2:18–32), and judgment (3:1–21)—are all taken up by the early Pentecostals (*Joel and the Spirit*, 12, 68–103).

areas of coherence between modern charismatic prophets and the Classical Prophets on the level of experience rather than content, this study will open up the wisdom of approximately one-third of the canon as a resource for contemporary Pentecostal praxis.

Conclusion

How does the practice of CP in the PAOC and PAONL cohere with the experience of the Old Testament prophets? This question cuts to the experiential core of Pentecostal worship: the practice of prophecy. This practice originated in the prophethood of Moses, was fully expressed in the eschatological prophethood of Jesus, and finds its modern expression in the prophetic community that was formed by the Spirit's outpouring on the Day of Pentecost. Paul's discussion of the gift of prophecy has provided Pentecostals with insight on how this prophethood operates. This research is expected to benefit a variety of audiences. Cartledge writes about three levels of discourse: "the ordinary, the ecclesial, and the academic."[76] This question will benefit the ordinary by providing laypeople with a way to understand and draw insight from the Classical Prophets.[77] It will benefit the ecclesia, specifically the PAOC and PAONL, by providing them more insight into the shifting nature of spirituality in their congregations. Finally, it will benefit the academy by providing qualitative research to fill a lacuna in the data on the Canadian expression of this religious practice.

76. Cartledge, "Locating the Spirit," 260.

77. Cartledge describes the ordinary as "the everyday reflective God-talk found among believers in the pews. It is the kind of theology found among members after the service, which, over coffee, they deconstruct the pastor's sermon, and sometimes they do this with knowledge" ("Locating the Spirit," 260)!

Chapter 1: Definitions and Method

This chapter consists of two main sections. First, the methodologies through which this topic will be researched will be defined, with attention given to how these methodologies interact with the subject matter and with each other. Second, the research procedure of this study will be laid out.

Four Lenses

1. Practical Theology

Practical theology has undergone a dramatic shift in recent years from applied theology to a more sophisticated academic field that seeks to account for the complex interactions between theory and practice.[1] Friedrich Schleiermacher brought practical theology into the university, ensconcing the traditional theory-to-practice paradigm. He used the analogy of a tree to describe his theological system. The roots of the tree represented philosophical theology, the trunk represented historical theology, and the crown was practical theology. Despite the "high and lofty status" Schleiermacher gave to practical theology, it had the functional effect of reducing it to a technical field—"an art or skillful craft (*Kunstlehre*, or *technē*, in the Greek sense) that links thought and practice."[2] While this had the positive effect of defining practical theology as a legitimate field of study in the university, there were two unfortunate consequences. First, the model divided theory from practice.[3] Second, practical theology became a concern only for the clergy—known as the "clerical paradigm."[4] This is clear

1. For a representative overview of the primary literature during this period, see Woodward and Pattison, *Blackwell Reader in Pastoral and Practical Theology*.

2. Crouter, "Shaping an Academic Discipline," 123.

3. Lum writes: "Theology became divided into speculative enquiry and practical application" (*Practice of Prophecy*, 16).

4. Miller-McLemore, "Contributions of Practical Theology," 13.

in Schleiermacher's twofold division of practical theology into "church service" and "church governance."[5] While many studies on prophecy exist using this applied model, it is the goal of this book to explore the ordinary level of discourse in order to understand how laypeople perceive and practice CP.[6] Consequently, this study requires a practical theology that holds practice and theory in critical correlation.

Stephen Pattison and James Woodward provide a useful definition of practical theology: "Pastoral/practical theology is a place where religious belief, tradition and practice meets contemporary experiences, questions and actions and conducts a dialogue that is mutually enriching, intellectually critical, and practically transforming."[7] In the theory-to-practice paradigm, religious belief, tradition, and practices (theory) would be *applied* to our contemporary experiences, questions, and actions. In Pattison and Woodward's model, these two sides relate to each other *dialogically*. Regarding CP, this means our interpretation of Scripture and the historic practices of the church (whether in first-century Syria or twentieth-century Southern Ontario) and our current experience of CP meet on a two-way street, where insight and inspiration flow both ways. Woodward and Pattison describe the dialogue between theory and practice in three ways: mutually enriching, intellectually critical, and practically transforming.[8] This dialogue is *mutually enriching* because just as a careful interpretation of Scripture can enrich contemporary spiritual practices, the subjective experience of God can conversely aid in the interpretation of Scripture. While this is controversial in some evangelical circles, it is commonly recognized in practical theology as well as Pentecostal hermeneutics. The experience of Spirit baptism with associated spiritual phenomena has provided the church with an enriched

5. Crouter, "Shaping an Academic Discipline," 124.

6. Studies using the applied model include: Fee, "Gifts of the Spirit"; Gee, *Concerning Spiritual Gifts*; Grudem, *Gift of Prophecy*; Robeck, "Prophecy"; and Turner, *Holy Spirit*.

7. Pattison and Woodward, "Introduction to Pastoral and Practical Theology," 7. There is no definitive definition of practical theology. Another popular definition comes from John Swinton and Harriet Mowat. They argue that practical theology is "critical, theological reflection on the practices of the Church as they interact with the practices of the world, with a view to ensuring and enabling faithful participation in God's redemptive practices in, to and for the world" (*Practical Theology and Qualitative Research*, 7). This definition adds a helpful missional note to the field but narrows the field unnecessarily by insisting that all practices of the Church must interact with the practices of the world. While CP does have a missional overtone (see 1 Cor 14:24), its main function is to build up the church.

8. Woodward and Pattison, "Introduction to Pastoral and Practical Theology," 7.

understanding of Acts. Bradley Truman Noel calls this the "Pentecostal Edge" by suggesting that "the Holy Spirit enables the reader to bridge the gap between the ancient authors of Scripture and the present interpreter. Pentecostals contribute most substantially to hermeneutics in the area of experience and verification."[9] This is memorably put in layman terms by Harvey Cox, who writes that for Pentecostals, "the man with an experience is never at the mercy of a man with a doctrine."[10] The dialogue between theory and practice must also be *intellectually critical*. This is to be expected on the theoretical side: exegetical and historical work have long been considered a rigorous science. For practical theologians, the empirical side of the research must be equally rigorous for the dialogue between theory and practice to be more than one-sided. Cartledge championed empirical theology in his pioneering work on CP in the 1980s and has since developed a robust theoretical framework to support it.[11] Finally, the dialogue is *practically transforming*. This is the ultimate goal of this research—that our understanding of the Old Testament prophets and our current practice of CP would be transformed by bringing theory and practice into conversation with each other in a rigorous reflective manner.

Practical theology is an ideal perspective from which to study prophecy. This discipline has the tools to unpack the rich complexity of this foundational Pentecostal practice. It is able to support both the Pentecostal insistence on the priority of Scripture as well as personal experience. Practical theology thrives in a multidisciplinary environment such as the study of CP where church history, biblical exegesis, and empirical investigation meet and conduct a mutually enriching, intellectually critical, and practically transforming dialogue.

There is one notable challenge regarding Pentecostalism and practical theology. Cartledge observed that many academic practical theologians use Scripture minimally if at all.[12] Some even treat the Bible as a problem to overcome. Rosemary Radford Ruether and the women-church movement, for example, have created alternative liturgies such as the exorcism

---

9. Noel, *Pentecostal and Postmodern Hermeneutics*, 164–65. Pentecostal scholarship has devoted significant effort to the role of experience in hermeneutics. For more on this theme, see Yong, *Spirit-Word-Community*, and Archer, *Pentecostal Hermeneutic*.

10. Cox, *Fire from Heaven*, 57.

11. See especially Cartledge, *Practical Theology*.

12. Cartledge, *Mediation of the Spirit*, 34–41.

of patriarchal texts from Scripture.[13] In an effort to overcome the scarcity of Scripture in much of practical theology, Cartledge constructively offered five dimensions to a practical theological reading of Scripture. First, such a reading will be *"hermeneutically reflexive."*[14] Practical theologians must declare their theological presuppositions. A charismatic theologian and a cessationist would shape and investigate CP in radically different ways. This straightforward confession of presuppositions aligns well with the phenomenological approach this study uses. Second, a practical theological reading of Scripture will "pay attention to the *explicit or implicit praxis of communities and individuals* described or inferred in the text."[15] It is not enough to know Paul spoke in tongues more than any of the Corinthian believers without considering the beliefs and theological assumptions that underlie Paul's praxis (1 Cor 14:18). Third, a practical theological reading will "pay attention to *agency and the relationship between the different agents* in the biblical texts."[16] This is particularly important in reflecting on prophecy since there is an incarnational agency portrayed. The relationship between the divine impulse and the prophet needs to be described. Fourth, a practical theological reading of Scripture "will treat the text as *holistic* and seek to trace trajectories across different genres wherever possible."[17] The *leitmotiv* of prophecy spans multiple genres from historical narrative to prophetic/apocalyptic, from gospel to epistle. An isolationist reading of key texts such as the ninefold list of 1 Cor 12:8–11 will not do justice to the redemptive purpose of prophecy throughout the canon. Finally, a practical theological reading will "consciously bring *contemporary questions and issues emerging from lived reality* to the text."[18] In order to do this, skill in both fields is required. Both "exegetical and theological rigor in the interpretation of texts and sociocultural sophistication in the mapping and reading of the contemporary situation"[19] are required if theological reflection is to be critically correlative.

---

13. Graham, *Transforming Practice*, 187–93.

14. Cartledge, *Mediation of the Spirit*, 45. Here and elsewhere, unless otherwise noted, italics are in the original.

15. Cartledge, *Mediation of the Spirit*, 45.

16. Cartledge, *Mediation of the Spirit*, 46.

17. Cartledge, *Mediation of the Spirit*, 46.

18. Cartledge, *Mediation of the Spirit*, 46.

19. Cartledge, *Mediation of the Spirit*, 46.

One final note is necessary regarding the relationship of practical theology with CP. Prophets understand themselves to be moved by the Spirit of God when they speak. This, of course, is beyond the realm of empirical study. How can anyone study God directly? Again, Cartledge is helpful in this area with his theology of mediation. While this is developed in detail in his *Mediation of the Spirit*, a summary statement from "Locating the Spirit" makes the point concisely.

> What we are researching when we include the Holy Spirit, is the person and work of the Spirit as *mediated* via Pentecostals in the testimonies to those experiences, in their narratives about what is going on, via the symbols that are important artifacts and events of such mediation as well the patterned action, the praxis of the communities, which are imbued with beliefs and values.[20]

I am a Pentecostal who believes the Spirit of God is active in the world today and speaks through the prophetic community of believers. However, the research will focus on the generative interaction—the dialogue—between the testimonies of modern-day charismatic prophets and the ancient testimony of the Old Testament prophets.

2. Practice-Led Research

The second methodology through which this study will be viewed is practice-led research (PLR). It is challenging to apply PLR to theological investigation. First, PLR is a relatively new form of research and, as such, is still developing its definitions and methodologies. Furthermore, PLR was developed as a way to integrate art schools into the tertiary-education sector.[21] There are few examples of PLR projects in the theological field and even fewer that focus on methodology.[22] Despite the challenges, PLR presents a meta-framework for uncovering new knowledge that is particularly useful for theologians rooted in the ecclesia. Linda Candy presents an operative definition of practice-led research with a number of key features: "Practice-led Research is concerned with the nature of practice and leads to new knowledge that has operational significance for that practice. The main focus of PLR is to advance knowledge about practice,

20. Cartledge, "Locating the Spirit," 259.
21. Gray, "Inquiry through Practice," 1.
22. Fergusson's "Practice-Led Theology" is a valuable exception.

or to advance knowledge within practice. Such research includes practice as an integral part of its method."[23]

Three key elements of Candy's definition apply directly to the study of CP. First, PLR is "concerned with the nature of practice."[24] This is precisely where my research focuses—the nature of CP as practiced by the PAOC. In this way, PLR resonates well with practical theology since both lenses take "people's experiences seriously as data for theological reflection, analysis, and thought."[25] Second, PLR "leads to new knowledge that has operational significance."[26] The research in this book will provide Pentecostal leaders with a rich picture of CP that will in turn enable them to transcend narrow presuppositions about the practice and to become more effective in their leadership. Finally, PLR must include "practice as an integral part of its method."[27] Since my own practice forms part of the research methodology, a brief overview of my professional practice is in order. As a PAOC ordained minister with over twenty years of pastoral experience in a variety of churches, as well as a former Western Ontario District section pastor[28] with oversight of churches in the Muskoka Section, I am in a strong position to study the phenomenon of CP. I have experienced CP from every angle: as a spokesperson, a congregant receiving the message, and a worship leader facilitating the corporate expression. The emphasis on self-reflexivity embedded in PLR will make my own experience integral to the research. This will become evident in the project design.

3. Phenomenological Research

Phenomenology is a method of philosophical investigation that was developed in the early twentieth century by Edmund Husserl. In the decades that followed, various philosophers, including Martin Heidegger and Maurice Merleau-Ponty, developed and extended Husserl's work.[29] In recent years, researchers have developed this philosophy into a valuable

---

23. Candy, "Practice Based Research," 3.

24. Candy, "Practice Based Research," 3.

25. Pattison and Woodward, "Introduction to Pastoral and Practical Theology," 15.

26. Candy, "Practice Based Research," 3.

27. Candy, "Practice Based Research," 3.

28. A section pastor in the Western Ontario District of the PAOC was previously known as a presbyter.

29. Gallagher, *Phenomenology*, 11.

qualitative research method that seeks to find "the common meaning for several individuals of their lived experiences of a concept or a phenomenon."[30] As an approach to qualitative research, phenomenological research begins "with assumptions, an interpretive or theoretical lens, and the study of research problems exploring the meaning individuals or groups ascribe to a social or human problem."[31] The phenomenological research seeks to bracket those assumptions and theories in order to obtain a clear understanding of the phenomenon itself.

Max van Manen defines phenomenology as "a method of abstemious reflection on the basic structures of the lived experience of human existence."[32] Two elements of this definition need to be unpacked with respect to CP. *Abstemious reflection* means that "theoretical, polemical, suppositional, and emotional intoxications" must be resisted in order to understand the event.[33] As with any phenomenon, practitioners of CP create and adopt theories that enable them to interpret their practice. In initial idea-generation conversations with various ministry leaders, I have heard of a number of theories. One pastor believes the majority of what passes for CP in our churches today is simply "the overflow of a rich devotional life." Another pastor, when questioned about CP, immediately quoted the three features of prophecy Paul wrote about to the church in Corinth. For him, prophecy is only for the "strengthening, encouraging and comfort" (1 Cor 14:4 NIV) of the church. If the content of the spoken word does not fit those categories, he dismisses it as false. Still another pastor, with discernment issues top of mind, told me people in his church are instructed to come to the front and share the word with the pastoral staff before it is relayed to the congregation. "This shouldn't be a problem," he said, "since the spirits of the prophets are subject to the prophets."[34] Phenomenological investigation seeks to bracket post-event reflection like this in order to see, with wonder, the uniqueness of the actual practice.

Lived experience has a technical meaning in phenomenology. It refers to more than day-to-day life experiences. Rather, it is "the prereflexive or predictive life of human experience as living through it."[35] Merleau-Ponty

30. Creswell and Poth, *Qualitative Inquiry*, 75.

31. Creswell and Poth, *Qualitative Inquiry*, 61.

32. Van Manen, *Phenomenology of Practice*, 26.

33. Van Manen, *Phenomenology of Practice*, 26.

34. This is a paraphrase of 1 Cor 14:32 NIV.

35. Van Manen, *Phenomenology of Practice*, 26.

describes it this way: "The world is not what I think, but what I live through."[36] The essence of an experience cannot be discovered in theories that flatten and categorize—it is discovered in the event as it gives itself to us in its originary wonder. Phenomenology seeks to encounter the experience "before we take a reflective view of it."[37] In order to get at this prereflexive experience, phenomenological writers use the process of reduction that can be broken into two movements: the epoché and the reduction-proper. This was first developed by Husserl, the father of phenomenology, and then expanded, challenged, and taken in new directions by the many phenomenologists who followed, including Heidegger,[38] Sartre,[39] and Merleau-Ponty.[40]

The Greek word *epoché* means "abstention, to stay away from."[41] Husserl adopted the term to describe the process whereby our theories and reflective thoughts on the phenomenon are suspended or bracketed.[42] Van Manen describes four different aspects of the epoché. The heuristic epoché brackets the researcher's "attitude of taken-for-grantedness"[43] and encourages a renewed sense of wonder at the lived experience. For CP this means the researcher steps back in wonder that God would choose to communicate in this way. The hermeneutic epoché brackets all interpretation of the event whether psychological, ideological, or theological. For CP, this means shaking off the prejudice that allows the researcher to ignore the details of the event. The experiential epoché brackets "all theory or theoretical meaning."[44] For CP, researchers must bracket all theories, whether simplistic and comfortable or profound and scholarly, so the phenomenon may be encountered afresh. The methodological epoché brackets "conventional techniques and seeks or invents an approach that might fit most appropriately the phenomenological topic under study."[45] Inventing an approach is difficult since there

---

36. In van Manen, *Phenomenology of Practice*, 40.

37. Van Manen, *Phenomenology of Practice*, 42.

38. *Being and Time* is Heidegger's most significant work. *Basic Problems of Phenomenology* deals critically with Husserl's phenomenological perspective.

39. Sartre unpacks his phenomenon of being in *Being and Nothingness*.

40. *Phenomenology of Perception* is where Merleau-Ponty clearly defines his interpretation of phenomenology.

41. Van Manen, *Phenomenology of Practice*, 215.

42. Husserl, *Idea of Phenomenology*, 33–42.

43. Van Manen, *Phenomenology of Practice*, 223.

44. Van Manen, *Phenomenology of Practice*, 225.

45. Van Manen, *Phenomenology of Practice*, 226.

are no simple steps to follow. The reward, however, is a richly descriptive picture of the essence of the phenomenon.

The reduction-proper follows the epoché. Etymologically speaking, reduction comes from *re-ducere*, or "to lead back."[46] Once the researcher minimizes interpretive judgment through rigorous bracketing, the reduction "engages the reflective phenomenological attitude that aims to address the uniqueness of a phenomenon as it shows or gives itself in its singularity."[47] It is easy to be misled here by thinking this is the stage where we generalize and theorize about the phenomenon. To engage in this is to miss the point of phenomenological inquiry. Theories can be evaluated in phenomenology on the basis of whether or not they fit the prereflexive self-givenness of the phenomenon. Unlike grounded theory, however, phenomenology does not seek a new theorization of the phenomenon. This method of inquiry is appropriate in this research project because robust empirical-theological models of the phenomenon have already been produced.

The reduction-proper is when the researcher shifts from focusing on self-bracketing to the phenomenon itself. "The qualities of the experience become the focus; the filling in or completion of the nature and meaning of the experience becomes the challenge."[48] The researcher provides a composite description of the textural and structural components of the practice in the form of a written manuscript that conveys the essence of the phenomenon. In phenomenological studies, the actual writing is part of the discovery process that enables the researcher to wrestle with the topic and encounter moments of insight. This rich and textured description of the phenomenon will provide material to compare and contrast with the experience of the Hebrew prophets.

4. Theological Reflection

The final methodology that will be recruited to gain insight into the research question is theological reflection. Here, the results of the phenomenological study will be brought into dialogue with the Old Testament prophets. This step, which places a high value on Scripture, is uncommon in many practical theological studies, but is particularly necessary for Pentecostal scholarship, given how Pentecostals value Scripture.

46. Van Manen, *Phenomenology of Practice*, 215.

47. Van Manen, *Phenomenology of Practice*, 228.

48. Moustakas, *Phenomenological Research Methods*, 90.

Pentecostals have always placed a high value on the authority of Scripture. The PAOC's "Statement of Fundamental and Essential Truths" reflects this perspective. The second line of the statement, still part of the preamble, says the PAOC "takes the Bible as its all-sufficient source of faith and practice."[49] The first article of the statement on "Holy Scriptures" expands this claim:

> All Scripture is given by inspiration of God by which we understand the whole Bible to be inspired in the sense that holy men of God were moved by the Holy Spirit to write the very words of Scripture. Divine inspiration extends equally and fully to all parts of the original writings. The whole Bible in the original is, therefore, without error and, as such, is infallible, absolutely supreme and sufficient in authority in all matters of faith and practice.[50]

Furthermore, with direct implications for prophecy, this first article states that "Christian believers today receive spiritual illumination to enable them to understand the Scriptures, but God does not grant new revelations that are contrary or additional to inspired truth."[51] The word "contrary" is easily understood, but the word "additional" should be nuanced. Prophecy clearly *does* grant revelations that can be considered additional to Scripture in that they address the contemporary church. The intent of the PAOC's statement is to indicate that the practice of prophecy does not produce additional revelation on par with Scripture.[52] This official statement clearly sets the boundaries within which the gift of prophecy is expected to operate. Prophecy must always align with Scripture in order for it to be valid.[53] It should be noted that although the Spirit does not speak in a way that

49. PAOC, "Statement of Fundamental and Essential Truths," 1.

50. PAOC, "Statement of Fundamental and Essential Truths," 1.

51. PAOC, "Statement of Fundamental and Essential Truths," 1.

52. See Robeck on the limits of prophetic authority ("Prophecy," 1011–12) for an explanation of this distinction. In the information-gathering portion of this research project, the author did hear about a church that faithfully transcribed all the prophetic messages spoken in the congregation. This practice is unusual, but not contradictory to PAOC belief because the transcriptions were not perceived as an addition to the canon of Scripture.

53. A revised "Statement of Essential Truths" was adopted at the PAOC General Conference in May 2022. The new statement reaffirms a high view of scripture: "The Bible, both Old and New Testaments, is the written revelation of God's character and saving purposes for humanity and for all creation. As God's revelation, the entire Bible is true and trustworthy, and is the final and absolute authority for belief and conduct. The Holy Spirit who inspired the Bible enables its interpretation and application."

is contrary to Scripture, "the Spirit *does* work against our *readings* of the Scriptures, and against the assumptions, ambitions, and fears that energize those interpretations."[54] This is where the practical theological emphasis of mutually enriching dialogue is so important. It is possible that a careful empirical look at the practice of prophecy will challenge our interpretations of Scripture, thus enabling more faithful practice.

This high view of Scripture challenges the current practice of academic practical theology. Practical theologian Paul Ballard confesses that although all Christians view Scripture as a "fundamental authority," this authority is "interpreted quite differently."[55] Cartledge developed a sixfold typology of the way Scripture is used in academic practical theology and concluded that Scripture is rarely used in a substantial way.[56] The exception to this is the "sustained engagement" model.[57] In order for this research to benefit the PAOC, Scripture must be used in a way that resonates with their fundamental beliefs.

This study will follow Cartledge's "sustained engagement" model. The tradition of the Classical Prophets, especially Jeremiah, will be examined and key texts on the prophetic experience will be explored exegetically before they are brought into conversation with the findings of the phenomenological study. Ballard writes helpfully about the responsible use of the Bible in the process of theological reflection. First, "it is necessary to have sufficient acquaintance with biblical scholarship to be able to use the Scriptures with integrity."[58] That is the purpose of chapter 3—to explore in sufficient depth the current state of biblical scholarship on the experience of Jeremiah and the Classical Prophets. Second, it is necessary for the practical theologian to be "a member of the community of

54. Green, "Beautifying the Beautiful Word," 119.

55. Ballard, "Use of Scripture," 163.

56. First, some used an "*a priori conceptual grid*" that filters the way Scripture is used. Second, some theologians follow a "*proof-text approach*" that use passages of Scripture without regard to the contexts where those passages are set. Third, some use "*strategic selection*," choosing select key passages as a "motif to justify the standpoint of exploration and openness to theological reflection." Fourth, some scholars use a model of "*sustained engagement*," where a biblical passage or tradition is explored in some exegetical depth. Fifth, "one gets a sense that a number of practical theologians see the Bible as simply a huge problem for contemporary theology." This is known as the "*critical reading*" perspective. Finally, in the "*excluded approach*," some simply ignore Scripture (Cartledge, *Mediation of the Spirit*, 35–40).

57. Cartledge, *Mediation of the Spirit*, 38.

58. Ballard, "Use of Scripture," 168.

faith, its worship, fellowship, and witness."[59] Prayer and reflection within the context of the church community is a necessary feature both of theological reflection, practical theology, and PLR. Third, Scripture must be allowed, "in all its diversity and strangeness, become a companion on the way."[60] This requires imagination—a key feature that Walter Brueggemann identifies in the Old Testament prophets as well as in modern prophetic spirituality.[61] For Brueggemann, the prophets lived and acted *as if* the God of their ancestors was a real agent in the world. The juxtaposition of the shattering reality of God against the political and social realties of Israel inspired their messages—both of judgment and of hope. This imagination is stirred by God, empowering the "faithful interpretation of meaning."[62] This method will honor both Scripture and the context of the faith community that serves as the setting of this research.

The third chapter of this book, which focuses directly on the experience of the prophet Jeremiah, will follow a literary canonical approach. Interpretive approaches emphasizing the significance of the canon include Brevard S. Childs and James A. Sanders.[63] These approaches were formulated as a response to a problem: the historical analysis of Scripture was drifting from theological reflection. Sanders named his approach "canonical criticism," emphasizing the process by which the final shape of the canon was developed while Childs's "canonical approach" emphasized the significance of the final form of the canonical text.[64] Childs argues that "biblical texts are made relevant to today's community of faith and to the world, not by first decanonizing them in a claim of establishing an original setting, but by faithfully hearing the intent of the literature which has already been shaped to confront its hearers with the divine imperative."[65] This canonical approach to Scripture fits well with Pentecostalism. Kenneth J. Archer argues that early Pentecostals used a "canonical and text-centered synchronic

59. Ballard, "Use of Scripture," 168.

60. Ballard, "Use of Scripture," 169.

61. See his classic *Prophetic Imagination*, as well as his more recent *Practice of Prophetic Imagination*.

62. Patton, *Ministry to Theology*, 19.

63. For their key works, see Childs, *Introduction to the Old Testament as Scripture*, and Sanders, *From Sacred Story to Sacred Text*. For a description of how this approach developed and dealt with the canonical shape of the prophets, see Glazov, "Canonical Criticism."

64. Glazov, "Canonical Criticism," 78.

65. Childs, "Canonical Shape," 54.

approach" to Scripture that was later replaced by a historical critical method.[66] That shift in methodology has undermined Pentecostal identity.[67] A canonical approach resonates more closely with early Pentecostalism and is particularly suited for this study's audience.

The canonical approach to Scripture also fits well with a literary approach since literary approaches, by definition, analyze the literary form of the text.[68] A literary approach to Jeremiah views the whole text as a unity, despite the shifting subgenres of poetic oracles, prose sermons, and biographical narratives.[69] The literary approach also gives full weight to the artistry of the text, including the "powerful and provocative use of metaphor."[70] Like the canonical approach, a literary approach has also been suggested as an ideal fit for Pentecostal scholarship. Steven Jack Land argues it is the narrative nature of the Pentecostal tradition that unifies the diverse movement.[71] Any reformulation of Pentecostal spirituality requires engagement with the narrative of Scripture.[72]

66. Archer, "Early Pentecostal Biblical Interpretation," 45.

67. Archer, "Early Pentecostal Biblical Interpretation," 45. On Pentecostal identity, Archer writes: "This [shift in hermeneutical approach] has affected North American Pentecostal community identity—an identity that becomes less Pentecostal and more acceptable to mainstream rationalistic and politically Republican Evangelicalism" (*Pentecostal Hermeneutic* 201).

68. Beal notes that while "attention to diachronic, historical questions at times informs the investigation, its focus remains upon the final form of the text" (Beal, "Literary Approaches," 506).

69. Rosenberg points out a paradox in a literary approach to Jeremiah. The poetic material is more closely identified with Jeremiah's own voice but does not include biographical detail. The biographical detail, while illuminative, takes the reader away from the prophet's own utterances ("Jeremiah and Ezekiel," 184).

70. Brueggemann, *Commentary on Jeremiah*, 16. Brueggemann goes on to highlight some of these metaphors: "Through its concrete language the text of Jeremiah can variously evoke a sense of creation that has massively regressed to chaos (4:23–26), an awareness of God's grief and sickness at Judah's obduracy (8:18—9:3), or the resumption of wedding parties in a land where all such social rejoicing had stopped (33:11; cf. 7:34; 16:9; 25:10)" (*Commentary on Jeremiah*, 16).

71. Land, *Pentecostal Spirituality*, 222.

72. It should be noted that Land was concerned primarily with "the biblical account of Pentecost, the present reality, [and] the apocalyptic goal" (*Pentecostal Spirituality*, 222–23). That said, it is my hope that this book will connect the Pentecostal narrative more firmly to the Old Testament prophets, thus expanding the nature of Pentecostal's narrative self-understanding.

Research Procedure

With the phenomenon of CP roughly defined and methodological parameters in place, it is now time to clearly lay out the procedure this study follows. The project consists of five steps. These steps take into consideration the unique features of the four methodologies presented above and provide an answer to the question: *How does the practice of CP in the PAOC and PAONL cohere with the experience of the Old Testament prophets?*

In chapter 2, a review is conducted on both the theoretical and empirical literature on prophecy. Theoretical literature refers to research conducted on textual sources, while empirical literature refers to practical theological explorations of practice. Due to the abundance of literature on the Old Testament prophets, this literature review was guided strictly by the research question, focusing specifically on areas of coherence or tension between the Old Testament and modern CP. The literature review provides a fulsome picture of CP as it is understood academically and practically in global perspective. A literature review sits in uneasy tension with a phenomenological methodology that seeks to bracket all theoretical reflection in the epoché. To address this concern, the literature review was completed before the start of the phenomenological interviews to facilitate the exposure and intentional bracketing process.

In chapter 3, the experience of the Old Testament prophets is explored with special focus on Jeremiah. To be clear, prophetic experience does not involve the *content* of the prophetic messages. To attempt this would miss the point of connection between the Old Testament and charismatic prophets. Muindi argued that the "perlocutionary effect of a prophetic utterance is more than the illocutionary intention that is conveyed in the content of the message."[73] In CP, the sacramental nature of the phenomenon is just as significant as the content of the message. Jeremiah is the obvious choice for the focus of this study because "unlike any other prophetic work, the book of Jeremiah concentrates dramatically on the figure of the prophet himself."[74]

---

73. Muindi, "Nature and Significance," 242. Briggs also draws on speech-act theory to describe the performative nature of the prophetic experience: "Prophetic texts describe some aspects of reality but also serve to bring about other aspects" so that the content of an oracle "is an illocutionary act, taking place in the pronouncing of the worlds" but the actual responses of the prophet's audience "is perlocutionary, contingent upon the real-world vagaries of human response to the oracle" (Briggs, "Hermeneutics," 326).

74. Smith, *Laments of Jeremiah*, 1.

Jeremiah's experience will provide rich data that can be brought into dialogue with the experience of modern-day charismatic prophets.

Chapter 4 is a phenomenological study of CP in the PAOC and PA-ONL. The research followed Clark Moustakas's methodology as described in *Phenomenological Research Methods*. In phenomenological research, all *a priori* theories, presuppositions, and interpretive frameworks should be bracketed insofar as possible. This is admittedly a difficult thing to accomplish since, given the PLR perspective, the researcher participates in the practice that is under phenomenological investigation. Jeanne J. LeVasseur provides a helpful perspective on the difficulty of bracketing. She emphasizes the role of curiosity in bracketing the natural attitude. In bracketing, the researcher is able to "get beyond ordinary assumptions of understanding and stay persistently curious about new phenomena."[75] By intentionally setting presuppositions aside, the phenomenon of CP will be experienced in "fresh experience and the possibility of new horizons of meaning."[76] In order to facilitate this bracketing, I began by writing out and reflecting on my own experience with the phenomenon of CP.[77]

Next, a diverse group of eight research participants with experience in CP was chosen from across Canada.[78] The phenomenological interview was then used to explore each participant's experience with CP. Following this, I transcribed the interviews, creating a textual source to begin the identification of textural and structural components.[79] From these manuscripts, all relevant statements of each participant were placed in a chart. As the chart was populated, "invariant meaning units" became evident.[80] Through the clustering of meaning units and the writing and rewriting process, textural and structural elements were identified and described with many "verbatim examples."[81] Finally, a "textural-structural" (or composite) description of the phenomenon was written.[82]

75. LeVasseur, "Bracketing in Phenomenology," 419.

76. LeVasseur, "Bracketing in Phenomenology," 419.

77. Creswell and Poth, *Qualitative Inquiry*, 77.

78. This project received approval from the McMaster Research Ethics Board for research on human subjects.

79. Textural components refer to the "'what' of the appearing phenomenon" while structural components refer to the elements that "underlie textures and are inherent in them" (Moustakas, *Phenomenological Research Methods*, 78–79).

80. Moustakas, *Phenomenological Research Methods*, 122.

81. Moustakas, *Phenomenological Research Methods*, 122.

82. Moustakas, *Phenomenological Research Methods*, 122.

In chapter 5, the experience of the Old Testament prophets and modern charismatic prophets are brought into dialogue to directly answer the research question, *How does the practice of CP in the PAOC and PAONL cohere with the experience of the Old Testament prophets?* This is where Pattison and Woodward's mutually enriching dialogue of practical theology will take place. The experience of the Old Testament prophets will be viewed alongside the experience of current practitioners of CP not as a model or framework, but as additional study subjects.

In the sixth and final chapter, I will summarize the research findings and point out significant conclusions. The limits of this study will be clearly laid out and areas for future study noted. This study will provide the academy with new qualitative research on a significant religious practice of Pentecostals. The PAOC will benefit from a deeper understanding of what is being practiced in their own churches. Finally, ordinary laypeople will be able to view their spiritual worship practices as standing in a long line of prophets rooted ultimately in their Jewish heritage.

Chapter 2: Literature Review

Theological and Empirical

PROPHECY IS A MULTIFACETED topic. Areas for investigation cover the gamut from historical studies on the ancient Near East to biblical studies, including the Old and New Testaments, to modern sociological and ethnographic studies. Literature on these topics is correspondingly broad and multidisciplinary.[1] This literature review will narrow its focus to areas germane to the research question: *How does the practice of CP in the PAOC and PAONL cohere with the experience of the Old Testament prophets?* For the purposes of this study, New Testament prophecy and modern CP will be viewed synonymously.[2] This literature review will be divided into two broad categories: theoretical and empirical studies. Theoretical studies are studies that focus their investigation on textual sources while empirical studies focus their investigation on modern praxis using both qualitative and quantitative methodologies. All the empirical studies in this literature review are practical theological studies that reflect a nuanced critical correlation between theory and practice. The theoretical studies, when they

---

1. Helpful literature reviews on this topic include chapter 4 of Muindi's *Pentecostal-Charismatic Prophecy* (91–140) and chapters 4 and 5 of Lum's *The Practice of Prophecy* (86–157).

2. The reason for this is contextual. The setting of this study—the PAOC and PAONL—is part of a broad classical Pentecostal tradition that understands its charismatic praxis as a continuation of the praxis of the early church. While the truth of this perspective can be debated, that debate does not change self-perception. Robeck describes this self-understanding: "From the beginning of the modern Pentecostal Movement, Classical Pentecostals have understood themselves as standing within a very long prophetic tradition. When they think of the gift of prophecy, they think first of the Old, and then of the New Testament prophets . . . They acknowledge the continuation of prophetic manifestations throughout the course of the Church's history" ("Pentecostal Perspective," 109).

mention modern praxis, regularly assume a theory-to-practice paradigm.[3] That is, truth is discovered in biblical text and then applied to practice.[4] While theoretical and empirical studies are categorized separately, they do overlap. For example, Wayne Grudem's influential study *The Gift of Prophecy* suggests revised areas of praxis for the church.[5] On the other hand, each empirical study reflects theologically on the data their investigations generate using theoretical literature.[6] In this literature review, therefore, theoretical and empirical studies will inform each other where appropriate. With two exceptions, the literature does not explicitly focus on the relationship between Old Testament prophecy and CP.[7] Therefore, three categories from the theoretical literature and three categories from the empirical literature have been identified where Old Testament prophecy and CP can be analyzed for coherence or discontinuity. The three categories from the theoretical literature are: the intertestamental break and restoration of prophecy, Jesus as the fulfillment of Old Testament prophecy, and the authority of prophecy. The three categories from the empirical literature are condemnatory prophecy, the revelatory impulse, and prophecy as an intense sacramental experience.

Theoretical Studies

This section draws on material from biblical and historical studies to examine how Old Testament and New Testament prophecy are related. Three

---

3. Browning describes the theory-to-practice paradigm in his classic text, *A Fundamental Practical Theology*, 5.

4. As mentioned in chapter 1, this study operates within a practical theological framework that understands theory and practice as dialogue partners. Browning describes this view as one that "goes from practice to theory and back to practice" (*Fundamental Practical Theology*, 7). While the applied theological studies surveyed in this literature review do not always acknowledge the way that practice informs their exegesis, theological presuppositions can be discerned.

5. For example, Grudem advises those exercising the gift of prophecy in the church to avoid using the Old Testament phrase "Thus says the Lord" on the basis of his view that New Testament prophets speak *fallibly* what God brings to their mind (71–94).

6. For example, Cartledge reflects on sociological, psychological, and theological literature to interpret his empirical study of CP in the Church of England (*Narratives and Numbers*, 9–14).

7. The exceptions are both found in empirical studies. See Cartledge's analysis of Turner (*Narratives and Numbers*, 14) and Lum's review of Classical Pentecostal literature (*Practice of Prophecy*, 100).

themes have been identified to provide structure to this analysis: the intertestamental break and restoration of prophecy, Jesus as the fulfillment of Old Testament prophecy, and the authority of prophecy. Since this project is practice-led with a phenomenological study at its core, special attention will be given to literature created by Pentecostal scholars and literature that has had an impact on Pentecostal praxis. The immediate context of this study is the PAOC and PAONL, so the PAOC's position paper will be given special attention where it intersects with the three themes.[8]

1. The Intertestamental Break and Restoration of Prophecy

Perhaps the largest potential area of discontinuity between Old Testament and New Testament prophecy (and, by extension, modern-day CP) concerns the so-called silent years of the intertestamental period. The massive disruption of the Babylonian exile shifted the nature of every institution in ancient Israel, including prophecy. John Barton notes that "in time prophecy did gradually evolve into something very different from what had been known in preexilic Israel; and by the New Testament period the designation 'prophet' applied to people in whom very few of the characteristic features of the preexilic prophets are discernible."[9] By the time of Jesus, the idea developed that prophecy had ceased.[10] Of course, the *belief* that prophecy ceased is different than the actual cessation of prophecy. Whether or not prophecy ceased in the intertestamental period is significant for this study because a break may suggest that New Testament prophecy (and by extension, modern-day CP) is a substantially different phenomenon. Conversely, if prophecy continued throughout the intertestamental period, this strengthens the potential coherence between Old Testament prophecy and CP. This section of the literature review will examine support for and against the idea that prophecy ceased in the intertestamental period before examining Pentecostal views on the matter.

The belief that prophecy ceased during the intertestamental period is called the "early consensus" by Benjamin D. Sommer.[11] Evidence for this view is found in Jewish texts from the second century BC to the second century AD. The famine that followed the death of Judas Maccabeus is described as

8. The PAONL does not have an official published position on prophecy.

9. Barton, "Postexilic Hebrew Prophecy," 489.

10. Barton, "Postexilic Hebrew Prophecy," 489.

11. Sommer, "Did Prophecy Cease?," 32.

"a great distress in Israel, such as had not been since the time that *the prophets ceased to appear* among them" (1 Macc 9:27, emphasis added). Another example of this belief is found in the Jewish pseudepigraphical text 2 Baruch, written after the first-century destruction of the temple.

> Furthermore, know, then, that in former times and in generations of old our fathers had righteous helpers and prophets and holy men. But we were in our land, and they helped us when we sinned, and they interceded on our behalf with him who made us, because they trusted in their works. And the Mighty One heard them and forgave us. But now the righteous have been gathered, and *the prophets have fallen asleep*. We, too, have left our land, and Zion has been taken from us, and we have nothing now except for the Mighty One and his Torah. (2 Barch 85:2–3)[12]

This Jewish author laments the fact that unlike in earlier times, there are no prophets left to intercede with God on their behalf. This provides a rationale for why the Jewish people lost their temple and their land. A tannaitic saying quoted in *b. Sanh.* 11a reads, "The tannaitic rabbis taught: From the time that the last prophets . . . Haggai, Zechariah, and Malachi, died, the holy spirit was withdrawn . . . from Israel."[13] Sommer cites a number of other Talmudic sources to make the point that this opinion "reflects a widespread notion."[14] On the basis of this early evidence, Sommer concludes his study by claiming the cessation of prophecy was complete by the second century BC. "By the time of the Hasmoneans, true prophecy was largely acknowledged to have ceased."[15]

Sommer's "early consensus" has been challenged by a number of biblical scholars, including Ephraim Urbach, David E. Aune, Thomas Overholt, and Frederick Greenspahn.[16] Evidence that prophecy continued through the intertestamental period will now be considered. Aune cites examples from Josephus and from the Gospels to show that prophecy continued throughout the intertestamental period.[17] Josephus indicates that prophecy

12. Stone and Henze, *4 Ezra and 2 Baruch*, 140, emphasis added.

13. Sommer, "Did Prophecy Cease?," 33.

14. Other Talmudic sources include *b. Yoma* 9b, *y. Sotah* 48b, *y. Sotah* 9:13 (Sommer, "Did Prophecy Cease?," 34).

15. Sommer, "Did Prophecy Cease?," 47.

16. See Urbach, "When Did Prophecy Cease?"; Aune, *Prophecy in Early Christian and the Ancient Mediterranean World*; Overholt, "End of Prophecy"; and Greenspahn, "Why Prophecy Ceased."

17. Aune, *Prophecy*, 129–32, 137–38.

existed during Herod's besieging of Jerusalem in 37 BC. "Throughout the city the agitation of the Jewish populace showed itself in various forms. The weaker gathered near the temple and became divinely possessed [*eudaimonia*] and composed many oracles [*polla theiōdesteron . . . elogopoiei*] fit for the crisis."[18] During the Roman siege of Jerusalem in AD 70, Josephus indicates that a false prophet led to the demise of six thousand people who sought refuge by the temple.[19] Immediately after this, Josephus explains that "many prophets [*prophētia*] were planted among the people by the rulers to proclaim that deliverance from God should be expected, so that desertions might be lessened and hope might encourage even those beyond fear and precaution."[20] Although Josephus here labels the prophets as "false," their existence and acceptance by the people suggests a popular belief that prophets did still exist.[21] Aune also cites John the Baptist as a widely known prophetic figure in early Judaism. Two prophetic speeches are attributed to him: Matt 3:7–10 (cf. Luke 3:10–14) and Mark 1:7–8 (cf. Matt 3:11–12; Luke 3:16–17). While each of these speeches "[defy] categorization in terms of the major OT prophetic speech forms," John the Baptist is presented as a prophetic figure in at least six ways.[22] Sommer accepts these examples of prophecy but interprets their significance differently. Rather than a continuation of a tradition, they should be understood as the revival of a dormant tradition—a revival that was anticipated. "Although postbiblical Jewish texts consistently attest to the belief that prophecy is a thing of the past, they also suggest that it is a thing of the future. The end of days and the coming of redemption, they claim, will be accompanied by the return of prophecy."[23] Max Turner challenges the rabbinic dictum that prophecy ceased with Haggai, Zechariah, and Malachi as a misunderstanding of the

18. Josephus, *War* 1:347. Translation by Aune, *Prophecy*, 137.

19. Josephus, *War* 6:285.

20. Josephus, *War* 6:286. Translation by Aune, *Prophecy*, 138. Sommer concurs that documents from the end of the Second Temple period, including Josephus, refer to prophetic figures but understands these as the revival of a "dormant" tradition (Sommer, "Did Prophecy Cease?," 34–36).

21. It is notable that Josephus rarely uses this term for anything other than Old Testament prophets (Aune, *Prophecy*, 138).

22. Aune, *Prophecy* 132. The six ways John is identified as a prophet are: (1) his costume is modeled after Old Testament prophets; (2) he was filled with the Spirit; (3) he was introduced in Luke 3:2 with an Old Testament prophetic revelation formula; (4) he rebuked Herod for immorality like the Classical Prophets; (5) his message demanded repentance; (6) he addressed all Israel (Aune, *Prophecy*, 130).

23. Sommer, "Did Prophecy Cease?," 36.

ancient literature.[24] This literature includes a variety of other similar statements that make it clear to be a rhetorical exaggeration.[25] Furthermore, in the same passage that speaks of the Holy Spirit's ceasing in Israel, Hillel and Samuel the Small are identified as two people the Spirit rested upon.[26] Turner concludes by writing, "While the 'intertestamental' period may not have produced prophetic figures of the caliber of the canonical prophets, prophecy was by no means extinct."[27]

L. Stephen Cook offers a compromise between the early consensus that prophecy ceased and what he calls the non-traditionalist view that prophecy did not cease.[28] In his dissertation, he probed the debate over the intertestamental cessation of prophecy directly through a comprehensive analysis of the ancient texts as well as modern literature on which this view is based.[29] He concludes that, despite "ongoing assault" in the last few decades, "Second Temple Jews did, on the whole, tend to believe that prophecy had ceased in the Persian period."[30] However, the non-traditionalist viewpoint has raised valid points that prevent the early consensus from becoming one-sided. Revelatory phenomena did exist in the intertestamental period, and it is from this context that rabbinic Judaism and Christianity emerged.[31] Furthermore, the non-traditionalist view reminds scholars of the necessity to return to the ancient people to understand how they interpreted shifts in prophetic inspiration.[32] In the end, Cook admits that there is both continuity and discontinuity between revelatory experience between the Classical Prophets and the intertestamental period. However, since the ancients themselves indicated a shift in the mode of prophecy between the two periods, Cook concludes that it is more faithful to Second Temple Judaism to emphasize the discontinuity.[33]

---

24. Turner, *Holy Spirit*, 190.

25. For example, "'when Rabbi Joshua died, men of counsel ceased, and reflection ended in Israel' (*t. Sot.* 15.3)" (Turner, *Holy Spirit*, 190). This cannot mean that all reflection ended, but rather, Rabbi Joshua was a deeply reflective person.

26. Turner claims this on the basis of *t. Sotah* 13:3, 4 (*Holy Spirit*, 190).

27. Turner, *Holy Spirit*, 191.

28. Cook, *On the Question of the "Cessation of Prophecy,"* 192–94.

29. Cook, *On the Question of the "Cessation of Prophecy."*

30. Cook, *On the Question of the "Cessation of Prophecy,"* 192.

31. Cook, *On the Question of the "Cessation of Prophecy,"* 192.

32. Cook, *On the Question of the "Cessation of Prophecy,"* 193.

33. Cook, *On the Question of the "Cessation of Prophecy,"* 193.

The reason for prophecy's change during the intertestamental period is significant. Sommer offers two reasons. First, "preexilic prophecy was closely related to the institution of kingship."[34] Frank Moore Cross states it bluntly: "It is fair to say that the institution of prophecy appeared simultaneously with kingship in Israel and fell with kingship."[35] With no royal audience left, the institution of prophecy declined. It is important to note that Cross here refers to the *institution* of prophecy that thrived under the monarchy. This does not mean that prophecy as a phenomenon ceased to exist, but that it lost its institutional support.[36] Second was the loss of the "ideological and imaginative world in which prophecy functioned."[37] Exile and the destruction of the temple disrupted the "possibility of communication between God and human."[38] Although a clear line of continuity may be drawn between the preexilic and postexilic prophets, the exile set in motion a change that resulted in the forms of prophetic expression changing significantly.[39]

One of the key changes between the preexilic and postexilic prophets that continued into the intertestamental period was the role of the Holy Spirit in prophecy. The Spirit of God, rarely mentioned in the preexilic prophets, takes a leading role in the postexilic period transporting Ezekiel (Ezek 3:12; 8:3; 11:1, 24), inspiring Trito-Isaiah (Isa 61:1), and stirring up the leadership of the exilic community throughout Haggai and Zechariah (Hag 1:14; 2:5; Zech 4:6; 7:12).[40] Robert P. Menzies notes that in intertestamental Judaism, the Spirit was understood as "the source of prophetic

34. Sommer, "Did Prophecy Cease?," 45.

35. Cross, *Canaanite Myth and Hebrew Epic*, 223.

36. Perhaps a parallel can be drawn here between the loss of national support of prophecy and the changes that entailed and the loss of national support of the church in post-Christendom today. In both cases, religious practice shifted in expression.

37. Sommer, "Did Prophecy Cease?," 46.

38. Sommer, "Did Prophecy Cease?," 46. Sommer goes on to clarify that this is a phenomenological statement—although prophecy *could* occur beyond the temple, it was not part of Israel's regular experience. Cross underscores the connection between king, temple, and prophecy by highlighting the postexilic prophets Haggai and Zechariah. They are "the last flicker of the old prophetic spirit which briefly flared when Zerubbabel rose up as a pretender to the royal office" (*Canaanite Myth and Hebrew Epic*, 343).

39. For Barton, these changes included prophets expressing their oracles "as additions to existing collections, or even as whole new works falsely attributed to figures from the past, rather than speaking in their own persons as earlier prophets had done" ("Postexilic Hebrew Prophecy," 495).

40. Barton, "Postexilic Hebrew Prophecy," 493.

inspiration, a *donum superadditum* granted to various individuals so they might fulfill a divinely appointed task."[41] Sommer notes that in rabbinic Hebrew, the phrase "holy spirit" becomes a synonym for prophecy.[42] Turner, a Baptist minister influenced by the charismatic movement, emphasizes the continuity of Spirit-inspired prophecy throughout the intertestamental period.[43] Turner identifies the Spirit in the Old Testament not as a personal being, but as "God's *own* life and vitality in action."[44] The Spirit in the Old Testament acted as a "channel of communication between God and a human person" that came to be known in rabbinic Judaism as "the Spirit of prophecy."[45] Turner goes on to identify four ways that the Spirit of prophecy functioned in rabbinic Judaism.[46] First, the Spirit of prophecy gives *charismatic guidance*.[47] In this sense, the Spirit of prophecy does not inspire an invasive oracular utterance, but special guidance. Turner describes this as phenomenologically akin to what Pentecostals would refer to as a word of knowledge.[48] Second, the Spirit of prophecy provides *charismatic wisdom*.[49] A clear example of this is found in second-century BC Sirach.

> If the great Lord is willing,
>> he will be filled with the spirit of understanding:
> he will pour forth words of wisdom of his own
>> and give thanks to the Lord in prayer.

41. Menzies, *Development of Early Christian Pneumatology*, 48. Menzies then argues that Luke drew from this understanding of the Spirit in his writings whereas Paul added soteriological functions to the reception of the Spirit (*Early Christian Pneumatology*, 316–18).

42. Sommer, "Did Prophecy Cease?," 33.

43. Cartledge has noted that Turner's view of New Testament prophecy roughly coheres with Old Testament prophecy, with some notable differences, including a lack of distinctive forms and the immediate reception and delivery of a message (*Narratives and Numbers*, 14).

44. Turner, *Holy Spirit*, 5.

45. Turner, *Holy Spirit*, 6.

46. The date of the sources on which Turner bases his argument is significant. "While the term 'Spirit of prophecy' only became *regular* in the Targums (from the first-century BC to mediaeval Aramaic interpretive renderings of the Hebrew Bible given in the synagogues), it was used in the pre-Christian writing *Jubilees* (31:12) and in Philo (*On Flight and Finding* 186 and *Life of Moses* 1.227), and something like the *concept* denoted by the phrase 'Spirit of prophecy' (as used in the Targums) is older" (*Holy Spirit*, 7).

47. Turner, *Holy Spirit*, 8–10.

48. Turner, *Holy Spirit*, 9.

49. Turner, *Holy Spirit*, 10–12.

> The Lord will direct his counsel and knowledge,
>> as he meditates on his mysteries.
> He will show the wisdom of what he has learned,
>> and will glory in the law of the Lord's covenant. (Sir 39:6–8)

Turner relates this function of the Spirit of prophecy to Paul's prayer for the Ephesians, that God "may give you a spirit of wisdom and revelation as you come to know him" (Eph 1:17). Third, the Spirit of prophecy gives *invasively inspired prophetic speech*.[50] By "invasive," Turner describes those moments when the Spirit "comes upon a person and they are caught up and inspired to speak."[51] This differs from the usual form or prophecy in the Old Testament where prophets recount at a later time what the Spirit of God had revealed to them.[52] This mode of activity has more in common with Hellenistic Judaism than Palestinian Judaism, given the context of Greek-style mantic prophecy. While this form of inspiration was rare, it is illustrated in Josephus's recounting of the story of Balaam from Num 23–24:

> Such was the inspired utterance of one who was no longer his own master but was *overruled by the divine spirit* to deliver it . . . "Balak," said [Balaam], "hast thou reflected on the whole matter and thinkest thou that it rests with us at all to be silent or to speak on such themes as these, when we are possessed by the spirit of God? For that spirit gives utterance to such language and words as it will, whereof we are all *unconscious*."[53]

Finally, the Spirit of prophecy inspires *prophetic praise and worship*.[54] This gift associated with the Spirit of prophecy is rare, but "is the closest analogy in Judaism to the phenomenon of tongues on the day of Pentecost."[55] This understanding of the Spirit of prophecy is evident when the Masoretic Text of 1 Sam 10:6 is compared to the Targum. "The Spirit of the LORD will come upon you in power and you will prophecy with them; and you will be changed into another man" is changed to, "And *the spirit of prophecy from*

50. Turner, *Holy Spirit*, 12–13.

51. Turner, *Holy Spirit*, 12.

52. "If we are to judge by the example of Ezekiel, the prophet typically received his revelations and the content of his oracles in full some time *before* he delivered them to the people; it was perhaps only rarely a matter of *immediately* inspired speech or 'invasive' prophecy" (Turner, *Holy Spirit*, 188).

53. Josephus, *Ant.* 4:119, emphasis added.

54. Turner, *Holy Spirit*, 13–14.

55. Turner, *Holy Spirit*, 13.

before the Lord will reside upon you, and you will *sing praise* with them, and you will be changed into another man."[56] The change in the Targum indicates that the Spirit of the Lord is more fully understood as the Spirit of prophecy from before the Lord. Furthermore, the purpose of this inspiration is directly stated: to inspire praise. It is clear that Turner sees a direct line of continuity between prophecy in the Old Testament, the intertestamental period, and the New Testament. Turner's conclusion is clear:

> It is often held that Judaism believed in the complete withdrawal of the Spirit following the last canonical prophets, . . . a cessation that would last until the eschaton. This almost certainly rests on misunderstanding . . . It would be nearer the truth to say that many Jews thought experience of the Spirit of prophecy was relatively rare in their own day.[57]

Pentecostals have traditionally sided with the early scholarly consensus that prophetic activity ceased in Israel during the intertestamental times. Roger Stronstad states, "With a few exceptions (notably John Hyrcanus and a few Essene prophets), prophecy had ceased in Israel."[58] However, the reason he argues for this is significant. This silence is what makes the "outburst of prophetic activity" in the birth narrative of Luke's Gospel so significant.[59] The PAOC also agrees with the cessation of prophecy during the intertestamental time for the same reason as Stronstad:

> It was commonly held by many rabbis that God had ceased to speak to His people through genuine prophets. At the dawn of the New Testament era, the Jews found themselves once again under the heel of an occupying foreign power, the Romans. Into this environment God restores prophecy to Israel suddenly, dramatically and unexpectedly.[60]

---

56. Turner, *Holy Spirit*, 13, emphasis original. The word "sing" in Turner's translation is not in the Targum. However, this does not change the point of Turner's argument, that praise is an invasive event inspired by the Spirit of prophecy.

57. Turner, *Holy Spirit*, 14.

58. Stronstad, *Prophethood of All Believers*, 32. Robeck simply assumes the early scholarly consensus: "It is little wonder, then, that when John the Baptist appeared on the scene after some 300 years of prophetic absence, hordes of people went out to hear him" (Robeck, "Pentecostal Perspective," 116).

59. Stronstad, *Prophethood of All Believers*, 32.

60. PAOC, "Contemporary Prophets," 4.

The significance of Jesus as the fulfillment of Old Testament prophetic traditions will be examined in the next section.

In conclusion, it was originally assumed on the basis of the ancient literature that prophetic activity ceased in Israel with Haggai, Zechariah, and Malachi. However, many scholars now disagree with that view, suggesting that prophecy changed in expression rather than ceased. While Turner emphasizes the prophetic role of the Holy Spirit throughout the intertestamental time, Pentecostal scholars generally agree with the early scholarly consensus that prophetic activity ceased. This enables them to emphasize its restoration with Jesus.[61] A word of warning from the conclusion of Cook's study is appropriate here. "Regardless of which approach we take, our own presuppositions will of course, to some extent, emerge in the terminology we choose to use in our descriptions of ancient Jewish prophecy."[62] This is evident in how Pentecostals have stressed the cessation of prophecy in the intertestamental period. If Pentecostals seek to underscore the radical restoration of prophecy in John the Baptist and ultimately Jesus, then it is helpful to emphasize discontinuity and risk losing the thread of coherence that runs through the Old and into the New Testament.

2. Jesus as the Fulfillment of Old Testament Prophecy

All Christian theology is centered on Jesus—a truth that is amplified in classical Pentecostalism. The narrative shape of Pentecostalism is described by Wolfgang Vondey as "salvation, sanctification, Spirit baptism, divine healing, and glorification."[63] These five metaphors, however, were traditionally cast in Christocentric form and known as the "full gospel":[64]

1. Jesus saves

2. Jesus sanctifies

3. Jesus baptizes in the Spirit

---

61. While technically John the Baptist was the person who marked the restoration of prophecy (see Aune, *Prophecy*, 129–32), Pentecostal scholars emphasize Jesus along with the Gospel narratives.

62. Cook, *On the Question of the "Cessation of Prophecy,"* 194.

63. Vondey, *Pentecostal Theology*, 37.

64. Some Pentecostal traditions omit "Jesus Sanctifies." Thus, this description is also known as the foursquare or full gospel.

4. Jesus heals

5. Jesus is coming again

This leads Vondey to observe that although Pentecost is the symbol of Pentecostalism, "Jesus is undeniably the subject of the full gospel."[65] The intense focus on Jesus has implications for the relationship between Old Testament prophecy and CP. Jesus is both a point of discontinuity and continuity between the two eras in that Jesus is the fulfillment of all the Old Testament prophetic themes as well as the one who recreates the prophetic community by sending the Spirit. This section of the literature review will demonstrate how the expectation of prophetic renewal was fulfilled in Jesus before being passed on to the prophetic community.

As noted in the previous section, it was commonly believed that prophecy had either ceased or had evolved into something different in the years prior to the first century AD. Along with this belief came a longing for the restoration of prophecy as eschatological hopes increased under Roman rule. Turner argues that a major strand of Judaism expected the Spirit of prophecy evident in the Old Testament and intertestamental period to rest on the Messiah. He writes that first-century Jews "anticipated a Messiah mightily endowed with the Spirit as *both* the Spirit of prophecy (affording unique wisdom and knowledge of the Lord as the basis of his dynamic righteousness and 'fear of the Lord') *and* the Spirit of power (i.e., of the 'might' by which he asserts liberating rule against opposition)."[66] Sommer explains that this link between messianic expectation and prophecy is supported by the passage from Malachi where the prophet Elijah would return before the day of the Lord (Mal 4:5).[67] It was into this milieu

---

65. Vondey, *Pentecostal Theology*, 284. It is telling that one of the first major threats to the Pentecostal movement was the Oneness doctrine, a movement that emerged from the AG in 1914, "challenging the traditional Trinitarian doctrine and baptismal practice with a modalistic view of God, a doctrine of the name of Jesus, and an insistence upon rebaptism in the name of the lord Jesus" (Reed, "Oneness Pentecostalism," 936). It should be noted that part of the impetus for the Oneness Pentecostalism was modernity's shift to a low Christology. Pentecostals have traditionally held a high Christology, a view exaggerated in Oneness theology.

66. Turner supports this view by citing the Targum on Isa 11:1–4, using italics to show material the targumist added to the Hebrew text: "And a *king* shall come for the from the *sons* of Jesse, and *the Messiah* shall *be exalted* from *the sons of* his *sons*. [2] And upon him shall rest *the* spirit *of* might, a spirit of knowledge and the fear of the lord" (Turner, *Holy Spirit*, 19).

67. Sommer also cites a variety of other sources of this belief: "Sir 48:1–12; Matt 17:9–13; *Pesiq. R.* 35, end; *Gen. Rab.* 71:9; 99:11" ("Did Prophecy Cease," 37).

of prophetic expectancy that John the Baptist and Jesus burst into history. John the Baptist was the first prophet described in the New Testament, a "popular charismatic figure who created eschatological excitement, was alienated from conventional culture, was critical of the established authorities and suffered death at their hands, and had a community of disciples that continued to revere him after his death."[68] The Bible portrays John the Baptist as a figure in line with biblical prophets, but who was also "more than a prophet" (Matt 11:9). He was the immediate forerunner preparing the way for Jesus, the prophet *par excellence*.

Jesus is portrayed by all four Gospels as a prophet, but this identification is particularly nuanced in Luke.[69] For Stronstad, Jesus fulfills five different Old Testament prophetic motifs in himself.[70] Stronstad's fivefold rubric is a helpful way to collect how various biblical scholars identify Jesus as a prophet. First, Jesus is *the Isaianic Prophet*.[71] By this, Stronstad refers to Jesus' identification in the Gospel of Luke with both the prophet Isaiah commissioned in Isa 6 as well as the servant songs (Isa 42:1–4; 49:1–6; 50:4–7; 52:13—53:12).[72] Second, Jesus is *the prophet like Elijah and Elisha*.[73] Many of Jesus' miracles echo Elijah and Elisha's work.[74] Most significantly for this study, in the same way that the Spirit that empowered Elijah was transferred to Elisha when the former ascended to heaven, the Spirit of Jesus was transferred to Jesus' followers who performed many of the same signs and wonders that Jesus did.[75] Craig S. Keener draws

---

68. Boring, "Early Christian Prophecy," 497.

69. Boring, "Early Christian Prophecy," 498.

70. Stronstad, *Prophethood of All Believers*, 38–47.

71. Stronstad, *Prophethood of All Believers*, 38–40.

72. Jesus self-identified with Luke most explicitly in the synagogue at Nazareth (Luke 4:16–30). For a more detailed look at the connection between Isaiah's servant and Jesus, see Brown, "Jesus Messiah."

73. Stronstad, *Prophethood of All Believers*, 40–42.

74. For example: Both Jesus, Elijah, and Elisha cleansed lepers (Luke 5:12, 2 Kgs 5:8–14), controlled nature (Luke 8:22–25; 1 Kgs 17:1; 2 Kgs 2:8, 14, 19–22), multiplied food (Luke 9:10–17; 1 Kgs 17:16; 2 Kgs 4:3–7, 42–44), and most significantly, raised the dead (Luke 7:11–17; 9:49–56; 1 Kgs 17:17–24; 2 Kgs 4:34–39). Dubovský agrees that "Jesus performed the same types of miracles as Elijah and Elisha," although different types of miracles are emphasized (Dubovský, "From Miracle-Makers," 38). For a broader look at the internarratival connections between Elijah, Elisha, and Jesus, see Huddleston, "What Would Elijah and Elisha Do?"

75. This transfer motif is also visible in the Moses narrative. When Moses gathered the seventy elders of Israel, the Lord took "some of the spirit" that was on Moses and placed

this connection, noting that the presence of fire and wind at Pentecostal also accompanied Elijah's ascension.[76] Third, Jesus is *the rejected prophet*, recapitulating a "longstanding tradition" in the Old Testament.[77] Jesus self-consciously reflects on this theme in Luke 13:33–44 when he mourns the city that kills the prophets. Fourth, Jesus is *the prophet like Moses*.[78] Moses was Israel's paradigmatic prophet who prophesied about one coming after him to take his place (Deut 18:15; 34:10). Luke's account of the transfiguration indicates that Jesus is this prophet (Luke 9:28–36).[79] J. Severino Croatto notes how this "Christological rereading" of Deuteronomy is confirmed in Acts 3:22–24, where Luke explicitly identifies Jesus in the language of Deut 18:15.[80] Fifth, Jesus is *the royal prophet*.[81] These two themes of Jesus as prophet and king are comingled throughout Luke's gospel.[82] Awareness of Jesus' royal identity increases as he approaches his crucifixion, though he simultaneously ministers as a prophet. Crucified under the inscription, "King of the Jews" (Luke 23:38), he is recognized after his resurrection clearly as a prophet approved by God although rejected by chief priests and leaders (Luke 24:19–20). Croatto argues that these two themes sum up the description of Jesus in Luke-Acts as a whole. "The third Gospel portrays an active Jesus Prophet, and the book of Acts,

---

it on the elders (Num 11:17). When the Lord did this, "when the spirit rested upon them, they prophesied" (Num 11:25). This event is clearly echoed on the Day of Pentecost when the Spirit was poured out on believers and they prophesied (Acts 2:1–36).

76. Keener, *Acts*, 1:801.

77. Stronstad, *Prophethood of All Believers*, 42–44. For summary statements of this attitude, see 2 Kgs 17:13–14 and 2 Chr 36:15–16. Green also acknowledges this prophetic tradition: "Elsewhere in the Lukan narrative the motif of the suffering of the prophets has already surfaced, drawing on a long-standing tradition regarding the destiny of the prophets to undergo persecution and martyrdom and applying that tradition to Jesus" (*Luke*, 536).

78. Stronstad, *Prophethood of All Believers*, 44.

79. Specifically, on the mountain, Jesus appeared with Moses and Elijah. Jesus "became dazzling white" (Luke 9:29), echoing Moses' experience on Mount Sinai (Exod 34:29). More tellingly, a voice from the cloud during the transfiguration said, "This is my Son, my Chosen; listen to him" (Luke 9:35)! This is a clear literary response to Moses' prophecy, "The Lord your God will raise up for you a prophet like me from among your own people; *you shall heed such a prophet*" (Deut 18:15, emphasis added).

80. Croatto, "Jesus, Prophet like Elijah," 460–65.

81. Stronstad, *Prophethood of All Believers*, 44–47.

82. In the birth narratives, an angel tells Mary her son will receive "the throne of his ancestor David" (Luke 1:32). He is recognized by a blind beggar as the "Son of David" (Luke 18:38).

a Jesus Messiah (seated as a king at the right hand of God [Acts 2:33]) proclaimed in the kerygma."[83] In the end, you have a picture of Jesus as the descendant of King David, yet something greater.

By summing up each of these prophetic themes in himself, Jesus is presented by the gospel authors (and especially by Luke) as the fulfillment and ultimate representation of the Old Testament prophetic tradition. This, read in isolation, would emphasize the discontinuity between Old and New Testaments. Since Jesus has fulfilled the Old Testament prophetic motifs and has inaugurated the new covenant, should Christians understand prophecy today as something radically different? It is more helpful to view Jesus metaphorically as the singularity where all the prophetic themes of the Old Testament find their final expression before they again burst forth into the new covenant. M. Eugene Boring notes how in the early church it was believed that "the Spirit was given to the body of believers as a whole, and not only to gifted individuals within it."[84] This emphasis on the transfer of prophetic inspiration is anticipated by the way that Elisha recapitulated the ministry of Elijah once he received the Spirit of the prophet whom he followed. The transfer of prophetic inspiration from Jesus to the church is also anticipated by the story of the transfer of the Spirit from Moses to the seventy elders. Stronstad argues that this transfer motif is fully realized in the transfer of the Spirit from Jesus to the church:

> Luke portrays Jesus to be a prophet without equal or rival but not without successors, for Jesus concludes and caps his prophetic ministry by establishing his disciples as an eschatological community of Spirit-baptized prophets. In his absence they will minister by the same power of the Holy Spirit as he himself ministered by and will, therefore, do the same works as he himself did.[85]

Steve Moyise's observations underscore the theme of prophetic transfer from Jesus to the church in his analysis of the use of Old Testament prophetic texts in the New Testament.[86] It is regularly assumed that the Old

---

83. Croatto, "Jesus, Prophet like Elijah," 453–54.

84. Boring, "Early Christian Prophecy," 501. In the context of the article, Boring goes on to say that despite this belief, prophecy practically became the purview of an identifiable group of people who exercised the gift of prophecy. This does not, however, change the Lukan vision of Jesus as the one who gathers the prophetic themes in himself before pouring them out on all flesh.

85. Stronstad, *Prophethood of All Believers*, 47.

86. Moyise, "Prophets in the New Testament," 650–57.

Testament prophetic texts point to Jesus.[87] However, in terms of frequency, "the majority of texts are applied to the events that followed, particularly the birth of the church, the inclusion of the Gentiles, the present unbelief of Israel and future salvation."[88] This corrective reminds us that while the Old Testament prophets did point toward Jesus, their vision did not stop there. They are connected *through* the life, death, and resurrection of Jesus to the church—the body of Christ.

In sum, the literature presents Jesus as a prophetic figure who appeared in a context of prophetic expectation. He fulfilled at least five major Old Testament prophetic motifs in his life and ministry. After his death and resurrection, the transfer motif common to Moses and the seventy elders as well as Elijah and Elijah is used to indicate the transfer of the Spirit from Jesus to the church, the prophetic community. This suggests a continuity between Old Testament prophets and modern-day charismatic prophets through Jesus, the one who sums up and passes on the prophetic tradition.

3. The Authority of Prophecy

Classical Pentecostals hold a high view of Scripture. It is the "all-sufficient rule for faith and practice, . . . the infallible rule of faith and conduct, . . . superior to conscience and reason" (AG).[89] It is the verbally inspired Word of God (Church of God, Cleveland),[90] to which "none may add thereto or take away therefrom, except at their peril" (Elim Pentecostal Churches).[91] The adjectives applied to the Bible—infallible, inerrant, all-sufficient— have become banners under which Pentecostals have fought the specter of theological liberalism. The gift of prophecy directly challenges the privileged position of Scripture in the Pentecostal tradition. Do prophetic messages have *authority*? Are there levels of divine authority? How can Scripture be unique (and the canon closed) if any believer can speak prophetically under the inspiration of the Spirit today? This question of authority is a significant point of discontinuity between Old Testament and New Testament prophecy. The authority of New Testament prophecy

---

87. Indeed, this is what Stronstad argues in "Jesus: The Prophet Mighty in Word and Deed (Luke 1–24)," the second chapter of *The Prophethood of All Believers*, 28–47.

88. Moyise, "Prophets in the New Testament," 656.

89. Hollenweger, *Pentecostals*, 514.

90. Hollenweger, *Pentecostals*, 517.

91. Hollenweger, *Pentecostals*, 519.

(and, by extension, CP), is regularly minimized in order to safeguard the closed canon and the authority of Scripture.

Wayne Grudem has written directly about this topic in *The Gift of Prophecy*.[92] The concern to safeguard the closed canon is found throughout. This is evident in the way he frames the topic for a popular audience.[93] The first heading reads, "The Gift of Prophecy in the New Testament Church Had Less Authority than Scripture or Apostolic Teaching."[94] He ends this article by encouraging the practice of prophecy in church today. However, he cannot resist one closing caution:

> If the gift of prophecy begins to be used in your church, place even more emphasis on the vastly superior value of Scripture as the place where Christians can always go to hear the voice of the living God. Prophecy is a valuable gift, as are many other gifts, but it is in Scripture that God and only God speaks to us his very words, even today, and all through our lives. Rather than hoping at every worship service that the highlight would be some word of prophecy, those who use the gift of prophecy need to be reminded that they should find their focus of joy, their expectation, their delight in God himself as he speaks to us through the Bible.[95]

The rhetorical force of this argument ironically minimizes the gift of prophecy that Grudem sought to validate.

For Grudem, Old Testament Prophets spoke and wrote with "absolute divine authority," which is why they often used the words, "Thus says the Lord."[96] These prophets wrote their words as Scripture. To "disbelieve or disobey a prophet's words was to disbelieve or disobey God."[97] New

92. It is difficult to overestimate the significance of this work that is an expansion of Grudem's doctoral thesis, *The Gift of Prophecy in 1 Corinthians*. He first published *The Gift of Prophecy* in 1988, but it was reissued in 1988 and 2000, each time with significantly expanded appendixes. Grudem's work mediates between charismatics and cessationists. It is significant that both Packer and Wimber have written positively about this volume. Cartledge refers to Grudem's work as a "breakthrough . . . in the subject of NT studies" ("Charismatic Prophecy and New Testament Prophecy," 18).

93. The 2000 edition of *Gift of Prophecy* contains and appendix that reprints an article from *Christianity Today* where Grudem summarizes his argument for a popular audience (Grudem, "Why Christians Can Still Prophesy").

94. Grudem, *Gift of Prophecy*, 313.

95. Grudem, *Gift of Prophecy*, 327.

96. Grudem, *Gift of Prophecy*, 313.

97. Grudem, *Gift of Prophecy*, 313. Grudem nowhere in *Gift of Prophecy* mentions the process by which the prophet's words were edited and preserved as Scripture. In his first

Testament prophets do not have this authority. In fact, the very word "prophecy" had become watered-down in the New Testament era to refer merely to "one who speaks on the basis of some external influence."[98] For Grudem, people who prophecy in the New Testament are not speaking the inspired words of God, but rather "speaking merely human words to report something God brings to mind."[99] Grudem uses a series of examples to support this.[100] First, In Acts 21:4, Tyrian prophets told Paul "through the Spirit" to not go to Jerusalem. Paul disobeyed—something he would have never done had these prophets been speaking God's very words. Second, New Testament Christians are called to test prophecy and "hold fast what is good" (1 Thess 5:20–21). This implies that some prophecies "contain things that are good and some things that are not good," something that would never have been said of Old Testament prophets.[101] Third, Philip had four daughters who prophesied (Acts 21:9). For Grudem, this contradicts Paul's prohibition against women teaching in the church. Therefore, prophecy has less authority than teaching. This final reason is rejected by many Pentecostal traditions that hold an egalitarian position on women in ministry, including the PAOC.[102]

Further investigation of Grudem's second point, the testing of prophecy, will clarify the question of coherence or discontinuity between the Old Testament and New Testament prophets. To the church in Corinth, where Paul gave his most extensive treatment of the proper use of spiritual gifts, he says, "Let two or three prophets speak, and let the others weigh what is said"

---

chapter, "Old Testament Prophets: Speaking God's Very Words" (21–26), he conflates the original prophetic vocalization with the final canonical form when he says, "We could fully trust the words of the Old Testament Scriptures, and . . . we should fully obey its commands, for they are commands from God" (26). A fuller critical reflection on Grudem's view will follow below.

98. Grudem, *Gift of Prophecy*, 285. This understanding of prophecy is recognized in broader biblical studies. Boring notes that "a glance at the entry on 'prophecy' in the standard dictionary of ancient Greek (Liddell and Scott) will reveal that in the world where Christianity was born the terms *prophet*, *prophecy*, *prophesy*, and *prophetic* did not function univocally, but were used with reference to a variety of figures and functions" (Boring, "Early Christian Prophecy," 496).

99. Grudem, *Gift of Prophecy*, 71.

100. Grudem's full argument is laid out in *Gift of Prophecy*, 71–94.

101. Grudem, *Gift of Prophecy*, 316.

102. For the PAOC's position on women in ministry, see the "PAOC Statement of Affirmation Regarding the Equality of Women and Men in Leadership" that bases its theological reflection on the prophethood of all Spirit-empowered believers.

(1 Cor 14:29). While this point has been commonly interpreted to mean only two or three may speak prophetically during a service, Gordon F. Fee assures that this is not the case.[103] The limitation to two or three was to allow sufficient time for the worshiping community to evaluate the message before moving on.[104] In a series of short injunctions, Paul wrote this teaching for the church in Thessalonica. "Do not despise the words of prophets, but test everything; hold fast to what is good; abstain from every form of evil" (1 Thess 5:20–21). Pentecostals largely agree with the need to evaluate prophecy, although in practice this does not always occur.[105]

Another argument related to the testing of prophecy regards the consequences for false prophets. Deuteronomy states that "any prophet who speaks in the name of other gods, or who presumes to speak in my name a word that I have not commanded the prophet to speak—that prophet shall die" (Deut 18:20).[106] Thankfully, the death penalty is not suggested for New Testament prophets who speak falsely! Interestingly, Grudem has changed his understanding on the death penalty for false prophecy in the Old Testament. In the revised edition of *The Gift of Prophecy*, he indicates this change of perspective, noting that Deut 18:20 only requires death for those who speak a message God had not commanded *and* speaks in the name of other gods.[107] The problem is not a mistaken prophet, but one who speaks on behalf of foreign deities. "False prophets were known both by their advocacy of other gods and by the failure of their predictions to come true."[108] Even so, there is more leniency in the New Testament, where false prophets are to be identified and ignored—even though the world will listen to them (1 John 4:1–6).

103. Fee, *First Epistle to the Corinthians*, 693.

104. Fee, *First Epistle to the Corinthians*, 693.

105. Pentecostal scholars generally emphasize the significance of testing CP. For examples of this, see Robeck, "Prophecy," 1011, and Gee, *Concerning Spiritual Gifts*, 62–63. Lum admits that there are not enough studies on the evaluation of prophecy to make definitive conclusions. However, "the contemporary practice of personal prophecies raises questions on how the evaluation of such messages may be conducted, or if this is even done at all" (Lum, *Practice of Prophecy*, 138).

106. See also Deut 13:5, "But those prophets or those who divine by dreams shall be put to death for having spoken treason against the Lord your God . . ."

107. The conjunction between these two clauses is the Hebrew ו (or καί in the LXX). While modern translations use the word "or" to translate this conjunction (including CSB, ESV, NET, NIV, NLT, NRSV), Grudem claims the word should be translated with "and," thus supporting his idiosyncratic view (Grudem, *Gift of Prophecy*, 24, 274).

108. Grudem, *Gift of Prophecy*, 274.

It would appear that the role of evaluating prophecy and the consequences for false prophets is a clear area of discontinuity between Old and New Testament prophecy. Upon closer evaluation, the picture is not quite so clear. Grudem's distinction between authoritative Old Testament prophets and fallible New Testament prophets leaves some questions. In the first place, Grudem's insistence that Old Testament prophets had their words effectively dictated to them by God is questionable. Heschel speaks of prophets being caught up in the *pathos* of God, and authoritatively speaking God's heart in their language—an incarnational model of inspiration. "The prophet is not a mouthpiece, but a person; not an instrument, but a partner, an associate of God."[109] This is evident in books like Ezekiel where God's messages take on a priestly form—unsurprising given Ezekiel's training for the priesthood.[110] Furthermore, the Classical Prophets' messages are written in poetry with a discernible history of redaction that bears the marks of post-hoc editorial work.[111] Verbal dictation theory does not stand up to this evidence. Second, while Grudem asserts the infallibility of "a true prophet," he gives no consideration to the evaluative measures by which the Old Testament worshipping community would discern the true or false prophet. It is clear that these evaluations were made, whether correctly or incorrectly, by the recipients of the prophetic message. Thomas Overholt argues using the conflicting prophetic messages of Jer 27–29 that while there were no "firm set of criteria for distinguishing 'true' from 'false' prophets," that did not mean that such judgments were not made.[112] Overholt writes that when equally compelling prophets of Yahweh were in disagreement, "the key to the resolution of the problem lay in an interpretation of the people's religious heritage."[113] For Overholt, this testing process continues in the

---

109. Heschel, *Prophets*, 30.

110. For Ezekiel's Priestly background, see Tiemeyer, "Ezekiel."

111. Blenkinsopp explores the redaction history of the prophets in his classic, *A History of Prophecy in Israel*.

112. Overholt, "Jeremiah 27–29," 241.

113. Overholt, "Jeremiah 27–29," 241. In this specific case of Hananiah v. Jeremiah we see "the clash of two widely differing interpretations of the nature of Yahweh's action within Judah's present history" (245). While the message of both prophets could be considered true (244), Jeremiah's message was true for their current situation as well. The Israelites evaluated prophetic words "in the dual light of an affirmation about their religious heritage and a knowledge of the historical situation in which they lived" (248). The confrontation between Jeremiah and Hananiah will be examined in more detail in chapter 3.

New Testament, although the prophetic words are addressed more toward individuals than nations as a whole.[114]

In order to make the claim that New Testament prophets are not as authoritative as Old Testament prophets, Grudem offers a novel solution. He posits apostles as the successors to Old Testament prophets. "In the New Testament there are also people who can speak and write God's very words and have them recorded in Scripture, but we are surprised to find that Jesus no longer calls them 'prophets' but uses a new term, 'apostles.' *The apostles are the New Testament counterpart to the Old Testament prophets.*"[115] Prophets today, therefore should stop using the messenger formula, "Thus says the Lord," since it implies an authority the modern-day prophet does not have.[116] Grudem's novel solution to the question of the authority of New Testament prophets has drawn criticism from both Cessationists and Pentecostals. On the Cessationist side, Bruce Compton argues that Grudem's belief that New Testament prophecy is ongoing yet may be errant and lacks divine authority is an attempt to have the "best of two worlds."[117] Those occasions where New Testament prophets heard from God and "got it right" would undermine the closed canon.[118] On the other hand, Pentecostal scholar F. David Farnell identifies a number of weaknesses in Grudem's central argument.[119] Most significant is his assertion that the injunction to judge a prophecy "does not imply that the gift could result in errant pronouncements. The responsibility of New Testament prophets to weigh the prophecies of others does not imply that *true* prophets were capable of giving false prophecies, but that *false* prophets could disguise their falsity by occasional true utterances."[120] Ultimately,

---

114. Overholt, "Jeremiah 27–29," 248.

115. Grudem, *Gift of Prophecy*, 314, emphasis added.

116. Grudem, *Gift of Prophecy*, 318. Grudem goes one step further in minimizing the authority of New Testament prophets. After subjecting prophets to apostles who were able to write Scripture, he continues to argue that "prophecy has less authority than 'teaching'" as well (Grudem, *Gift of Prophecy*, 321). By way of contrast, Cartledge notes the value in charismatic prophets using the messenger formula. "Prophecy in the first person impresses the hearer with a sense of the immediacy of God" (*Narratives and Numbers*, 10).

117. Compton, "Continuation of NT Prophecy," 71.

118. Compton, "Continuation of NT Prophecy," 71.

119. Farnell, "Fallible New Testament Prophecy/Prophets?"

120. Farnell, "Fallible New Testament Prophecy/Prophets?," 178.

for Farnell, Grudem's solution to the problem of prophetic authority in the New Testament is "weak" and "unconvincing."[121]

Grudem's arguments aside, the belief that CP is not equal in authority to Scripture is almost universally accepted in Pentecostal traditions today.[122] Pentecostal scholar Robeck surveys various theological traditions on prophetic authority, before offering a robust statement on the value and limitations of prophetic authority for Pentecostals.[123] Robeck notes that many Reformed and dispensational theologians claim that Jesus is God's ultimate word to humanity on the basis of Heb 1:1–2. This, along with a cessationist interpretation of 1 Cor 13:10, renders any prophetic word today illegitimate.[124] The Roman Catholic doctrine of papal infallibility, though infrequently invoked, suggests a very high authority placed on prophecy, albeit under strict ecclesial boundaries.[125] Luther and Calvin interpreted the gift of prophecy as "a form of expository preaching or teaching," despite the regularly spontaneous nature of the gift.[126] In the end, Robeck concludes: "What is the limit of prophetic authority? Within the Christian tradition it must be limited by the teachings of Scripture as understood by the members of the community of faith as they seek to submit themselves one to another and to live under the guidance of Scripture as the ultimate written authority in all matters of faith and practice."[127] In this carefully nuanced statement, Robeck provides a hermeneutically

---

121. Farnell, "Fallible New Testament Prophecy/Prophets?," 179.

122. Lum states in his literature review that "prophecy should always be in agreement with Scripture and should never contradict it" (*Practice of Prophecy*, 136). This is confirmed in his empirical observations. 99.95 percent of Singaporean Assemblies of God surveyed indicated "Adherence to the Bible" as an important criterion in judging prophecy (*Practice of Prophecy*, 186). Robeck writes that "there is a clear sense in these [prophetic] messages that none of these words are intended to supersede or compete with Scripture in any way" ("Pentecostal Perspective," 133). The PAOC position paper clear states that the authority of New Testament prophecy "is of a different order" and is "not recognized as a canonical word that operates as the norm for God's people on the same level as the Scriptures" (PAOC, "Contemporary Prophets," 5).

123. Robeck, "Prophecy," 1011–12.

124. Robeck, "Prophecy," 1011.

125. Robeck, "Prophecy," 1011–12.

126. Robeck, "Prophecy," 1012. Muindi's research confirms the spontaneous nature of the prophetic gift in Kenyan Pentecostalism: "Charismatic prophecy is an invasive oracular utterance which arises from a perceptual immediacy of the divine presence" (*Pentecostal-Charismatic Prophecy*, 138).

127. Robeck, "Prophecy," 1012.

sound perspective on prophecy, acknowledging the role that the community plays in the interpretation of meaning.

The PAOC also offers a perspective that challenges Grudem yet comes to the same conclusion that New Testament prophecy is less authoritative than Old Testament prophecy. The PAOC states with Grudem that genuine Old Testament prophets were understood to speak the "very word of God."[128] These words were "recorded and given the highest level of authority, that of canonical Scripture."[129] However, in contrast to Grudem, the PAOC notes that these prophetic words "were ideally subject to theological and historical evaluation."[130] This evaluative process provides an area of coherence between Old Testament and New Testament prophets. In both eras, the words of the prophet were subject to evaluation by the faith community.[131] Despite this coherence, the PAOC does still argue for a difference in authority. The authority of New Testament prophecy "is of a different order. Contemporary prophecy is not recognized as a canonical word that operates as the norm for God's people on the same level as the Scriptures. Therefore it should not be presented in a fashion that associates every specific term or phrase to God or that demands unquestioned obedience."[132] While Grudem's rejection of the prophetic formula "Thus says the Lord" is not explicitly stated, the significance of subjugating the authority of New Testament prophets to scriptural norms is clear.

In conclusion, Pentecostal belief lines up with the broader church in regarding New Testament prophecy as less authoritative than Old Testament prophecy. This difference in authority necessitates clear evaluative procedures for New Testament prophecy. Although this is a significant area of discontinuity between the Old Testament and New Testament prophets, the influential work of Grudem overstates the issue. The PAOC

128. PAOC, "Contemporary Prophets," 5.

129. PAOC, "Contemporary Prophets," 5.

130. PAOC, "Contemporary Prophets," 5. The position paper contains no rationale to support this statement. Presumably theological and historical evaluation was part of the redactional process through which the Old Testament Scriptures were compiled and recognized as canonical.

131. Lum's qualitative study of Pentecostal pastors in Singapore revealed four criteria for testing prophecy. The most significant criteria was whether or not prophecy was in agreement with Scripture. Second, prophecies were evaluated to determine whether the message edified the congregation. Third, the Christian character of the person prophesying was examined. Fourth, the delivery of the prophecy was considered—was it done in order or did it disrupt the worship service (*Practice of Prophecy*, 77–80)?

132. PAOC, "Contemporary Prophets," 5.

along with biblical studies scholars such as Overholt believe that evaluative measures were taken in the Old Testament as well, even if they are not explicitly stated.

Theoretical Studies: Conclusion

Three areas have been examined in order to see whether or not there is coherence between Old Testament and New Testament prophecy: the intertestamental break and restoration of prophecy, the significance of Jesus as the singularity who sums up and passes on the prophetic tradition, and the relative authority of prophecy and necessary evaluative measures. This survey has shown that the question of coherence in the theoretical literature does not beget a simple answer. In each area, both continuity and discontinuity are evident. In the intertestamental time, there was a common belief that prophecy had ceased. However, this belief has been challenged by newer studies that emphasize the role of the Spirit of prophecy in the intertestamental period. In the first century, Jesus was identified as a prophet who summed up all the Old Testament prophetic traditions in himself before pouring them out on the church at Pentecost. This event can be viewed as a restoration of Old Testament prophecy for the followers of the Messiah, although subsequent expressions of prophecy were of a lower level of authority and required judgment by the worshipping community to which they were given. These explicitly stated evaluative measures are a change from Old Testament prophetic practice, although there is little doubt that the ancient Israelites also evaluated the prophetic words they received (whether they were correct or incorrect in their judgments).

In the theoretical literature, the question of coherence is a matter of emphasis that, in turn, is influenced by the theological presuppositions and intents of the writer. Broadly speaking, the theoretical literature overemphasizes the discontinuity between Old Testament and New Testament prophecy, an emphasis that influences the way prophecy is practiced and evaluated in the church today. This underscores the need for this research. To anticipate the following section, empirical studies will generally show a greater level of coherence between Old Testament prophecy and CP. The empirical research in this study (see chapter 4) will follow the trend, demonstrating a broad coherence between Old Testament prophecy and CP on an experiential level. This will serve as a corrective to the theoretical literature with its emphasis on discontinuity.

Empirical Studies

In contrast to the biblical and historical studies explored in the previous section, empirical studies focus on practical-theological work on CP. Four people have conducted empirical studies on CP: Mark J. Cartledge, Samuel Muindi, Dennis Lum, and Tania Harris.[133] Their research, focused on different contexts (England, Kenya, Singapore, and Australia, respectively), overlaps in generative ways. This literature review will survey ways these empirical studies frame the relationship between Old Testament prophecy and CP. Three themes provide the structure for this section: condemnatory prophecy, the revelatory impulse of prophecy, and prophecy as an intense sacramental experience.

1. Condemnatory Prophecy

There is a perceived shift in the content of prophecy between the Old Testament and today. The Old Testament prophets frequently uttered scathing rhetoric against other nations as well as against Israel and Judah.[134] In contrast, New Testament prophecy is regularly viewed as more encouraging in nature. In discussions about CP, 1 Cor 14:3 is commonly raised as a starting point.[135] "Those who prophesy speak to other people for their upbuilding and encouragement and consolation." Those three words—upbuilding, encouragement, and consolation—are then used to posit a difference between Old Testament prophecy and CP. While Old Testament prophets sometimes spoke words of condemnation, this is not viewed as within the purview of New Testament prophecy.[136] It should be noted, however, that not all interpreters use these three words to mean positive instead of negative. Grudem mentions that the first word—upbuilding—is also used in the New Testament to describe the result of

133. Harris's work is concerned more broadly with revelatory experiences (see especially her PhD dissertation, "Hearing God's Voice.")

134. Amos is an excellent example of this sort of prophecy. The book begins with prophetic judgments against Damascus, Gaza, Tyre, Edom, Ammon, and Moab, then continues with Judah and Israel using the same introductory formula (Amos 1–2).

135. Turner notes that "it is commonplace to begin with Paul's statement in 1 Corinthians 14:3 . . . that prophecy is for the edification, exhortation and consolation of the congregation" (*Holy Spirit*, 202).

136. See Cartledge, *Narratives and Numbers*, 1.

church discipline (2 Cor 10:8; 13:9).[137] Not everything that is upbuilding need be pleasant. Fee argues that upbuilding (he translates as edification) "controls the thought of the entire chapter."[138] It is within this context that the following two synonyms—encouragement and consolation—are situated. In sum, "the aim of prophecy is the growth of the church corporately, which involves the growth of its individual members."[139] This may occur through positive or negative prophetic "encouragement."[140]

The idea that New Testament prophecy differs from Old Testament prophecy in that its content is more encouraging is reflected in differing ways in modern CP. As indicated above, some modern practitioners apply 1 Cor 14:3 in a way that only allows for encouraging words to be spoken in the congregation. Perhaps surprisingly, the idea that prophecy can only be encouraging is not borne out by the fieldwork of Cartledge, Muindi, and Lum. In Muindi's research, 80 percent of participants in his case studies recall hearing prophetic messages that warned "against sin in the church," with 100 percent of his in-depth interview subjects reporting feeling a sense of "Godly fear" when prophesying.[141] Although this type of prophecy was less frequent in Lum's research, some still did report experiencing corrections, warnings, and even rebukes.[142] Cartledge notes that despite this type of prophecy being discouraged in general, it did appear "in many cases modelled on the Old Testament canonical prophets, with

---

137. Grudem, *Gift of Prophecy*, 126.

138. Fee, *First Epistle to the Corinthians*, 657.

139. Fee, *First Epistle to the Corinthians*, 658.

140. Robeck confirms the threefold purpose of prophecy in 1 Cor 14:3 but goes on to say that "prophetic gifts appear to have more than these three purposes" ("Pentecostal Perspective," 121). He cites divine direction as another purpose of prophecy.

141. Muindi, *Pentecostal-Charismatic Prophecy*, 240, 242. Evidence of condemnatory prophecy is most prominent in Muindi's work in Kenya. This may indicate a contrast between the therapeutic leaning of Western versions of Christianity in contrast to African spirituality. (For a description of the therapeutic nature of Western Christianity, see Brueggemann, *Mandate to Difference*, 63).

142. Lum, *Practice of Prophecy*, 188.

oracles in the first person singular."[143] In this example, CP coheres closely with Old Testament prophecy.[144]

2. The Revelatory Impulse

Empirical research on CP has described a variety of modes whereby people receive the prophetic impulse. This diversity reflects the diversity present in the Old Testament prophets, providing a strong area of coherence between the Old Testament prophecy and CP. Cartledge's study provides the fullest accounting of the various revelatory impulses.[145] This may be because his study was the only empirical study that did not focus directly on the corporate worship experience. Although he concluded that prophecy occurs "from the context of prayer and worship," he only informed his interviewees that "the subject matter under consideration was 'prophetic experiences' in general."[146] This broad approach yielded eleven modes in which the revelatory impulse was received by the prophet. This list is worth examining.

1. *Pictures.* While praying for a friend's marriage, the prophet saw a tangled heap of metal her friend could not sort out until a man with a blow torch arrived to help. The picture was interpreted as Jesus coming to do what the woman could not do to untangle her marital difficulties.[147]

2. *Words.* Either one word or a small phrase would come to the mind of the prophet, such as, "I will show you the way, remember I am always with you."[148]

143. Cartledge, *Narratives and Numbers*, 8. Cartledge's observation contrasts with Grudem's advice: "If someone really does think God is bringing something to mind which should be reported in the congregation, there is nothing wrong with saying, 'I think the Lord is putting on my mind that . . .' or, 'It seems to me that the Lord is showing us . . .' or some similar expression. Of course, that does not sound as 'forceful' as 'Thus says the Lord'" (*Gift of Prophecy*, 319).

144. This is an excellent example of where practical theology, understood as a mutually enriching dialogue between belief and practices, can inform both practice and belief. In this case, the practice of CP challenges common (mis)understandings of Scripture—CP is tied more closely to the Old Testament than current understanding would suggest.

145. Cartledge, "Charismatic Prophecy."

146. Cartledge, "Charismatic Prophecy," 79; *Narratives and Numbers*, 24.

147. Cartledge, "Charismatic Prophecy," 79.

148. Cartledge, "Charismatic Prophecy," 80.

3. *Inspired Prayer.* While praying for a contemporary event, the prayer takes on a new intensity as the revelatory impulse guides the person praying.[149]

4. *The Interpretation of Tongues.* A person asked God for healing, feeling despondent that God had not answered. She then began to speak in tongues. Following this "some words came into her mind which she believed were the interpretation . . . 'My child do not strive, just rest and rest in my love and grace and gentleness.'"[150]

5. *Dreams and Visions.* A woman sat in her bedroom and saw a cross made of light pulsating. She reflected on the vision and interpreted it as an exhortation from God for her to do the will of God while avoiding the things of the world. A Scripture (1 John 2:15a, 17b) guided her interpretation of the vision.

6. *Audible Voice.* A person was called to ministry when she explored churches in a new town. As she pushed open the door of the church, "a voice seemed to flow through my mind, which said: 'Your life will be closely bound up with this church . . .' It was audible enough to make me actually begin to turn around to see if there was anybody speaking."[151]

7. *Reception of Knowledge.* A person knew that he would have a motorcycle accident before it happened. On the day he knew the day the accident would happen he changed his route on the way home but the accident happened anyway.[152] (Perhaps public transit would have been a better choice!)

8. *Scripture Verses Coming to Mind.* During a Bible study discussion, one participant opened her Bible to Heb 10:25 and felt that God had given her the answer to the questions they were discussing.[153]

9. *Physical Sensation.* In this scenario a person felt pain in her chest while she prayed in a group for a person. She shared the sensation and they

---

149. Cartledge, "Charismatic Prophecy," 80.
150. Cartledge, "Charismatic Prophecy," 80.
151. Cartledge, "Charismatic Prophecy," 81.
152. Cartledge, "Charismatic Prophecy," 81.
153. Cartledge, "Charismatic Prophecy," 81.

prayed until the pain went away. Release from pain was an indication that God had answered their prayer.[154]

10. *Subjective Impressions.* This category covers those undefinable events that are difficult to describe. Some people have trouble trying to express how the divine impulse is revealed.[155]

11. *Compulsion to Speak Out or Write Something Down.* One person always prays with a journal at hand. On one occasion he felt like he needed to record a message: "Tell my people I do love them. There is no need to fear. I will guide them if they will but trust me."[156]

Dennis Lum's study indicates that the majority of prophetic impulses come in one of four forms: "a word or sentence coming to mind," "a general impression of what the message is," "a Scripture verse coming to my mind," and "an internal picture in my mind."[157] These four impulses line up with Cartledge's findings. The rarer prophetic impulses Lum identifies are "an internal voice speaking to me," "a physical sensation," "a dream," "an external vision before my eyes," "an external audible voice speaking to me," and "an angelic visitation."[158] Of these, angelic visitation (the least frequent prophetic impulse in Lum's study) was completely absent in Cartledge's work. As these studies indicate, there are a variety of ways that people receive the prophetic impulse.[159]

Cartledge and Lum, through a process of complexification, accounted for all the data in its rich diversity and illuminated the multiplex nature of CP. These identified prophetic impulses provide interesting areas of coherence with the Old Testament prophets. A quick survey of Scripture will show how the Old Testament prophets received divine communication in similar ways. These include pictures (Zech 4:1–6), words (Jer 1:9), inspired prayer (1 Kgs 18:36), dreams and visions (Ezek 1:4–28), audible voice (1 Kgs 19:13), reception of knowledge (Joel 2:28–29), Scripture verses coming to mind (Judg 6:7–10), physical sensation (Jer 20:9), a compulsion to speak out or write something down (Isa 6:8–10; Jer 30:2), and angelic

---

154. Cartledge, "Charismatic Prophecy," 82.

155. Cartledge, "Charismatic Prophecy," 82.

156. Cartledge, "Charismatic Prophecy," 82.

157. Lum, *Practice of Prophecy*, 182.

158. Lum, *Practice of Prophecy*, 182.

159. These revelatory modes should not be considered exhaustive. They are descriptive statements rooted in the contexts of the respective studies.

visitation (Isa 6:1–13). Of the two remaining modes that Cartledge identified, the interpretation of tongues is a New Testament phenomenon, while subjective impressions is too vague to clearly identify.[160] It is clear there is significant coherence in the diversity of revelatory impulses between the Old Testament prophets and CP.

3. Prophecy as an Intense Sacramental Experience

Classic Pentecostals have traditionally been reticent to describe experiences as sacramental (perhaps due to suspicions about Roman Catholic theology) but this attitude is changing.[161] Muindi makes use of the category of sacrament to describe CP by tracing the etymology of sacrament from the Latin *sacramentum* to the Greek μυστήριον, that is often translated in English as "mystery."[162] The Greek μυστήριον is used "in reference to divine mysteries in revelatory encounters," the prime mystery being the Incarnation of Jesus (1 Tim 3:16).[163] Thus, it is a natural word to refer to CP, where those present experience the immediacy of the divine presence.

Muindi describes CP as

> an intense moment of participatory interface between the divine spirit (the Holy Spirit) and the human deep unconscious dimension (the human spirit) and that the divine spirit overwhelmed and infused the human conscious dimension (the mind) with revelatory impulses. Such an intense participation of the human spirit in the divine Spirit is deemed to be a sacramental experience.[164]

160. In a study on the prophet Balaam (Num 22–24), Gass notes that the prophet received divine communication in five different modes: Balaam was tested through interaction with an angel, God "comes" to the prophet, the prophet "meets" God, the prophet becomes God's mouthpiece, and the prophet "sees" ("Modes of Divine Communication in the Balaam Narrative"). This again underscores the multiplicity of modes through which divine communication occurred in the Old Testament.

161. Hollenweger describes the fraught relationship between Pentecostalism and Roman Catholicism in *Pentecostalism*, 144–81. The PAOC has referred to the Lord's Supper and Water Baptism as "ordinances," not sacraments ("Statement of Fundamental and Essential Truths," 4). Wolfgang Vondey and Chris Green are among those Pentecostal scholars who use the category of sacraments, untying them from specific rituals and applying them to the whole of Christian life (Vondey and Green, "Between This and That").

162. Muindi, *Pentecostal-Charismatic Prophecy*, 189.

163. Muindi, *Pentecostal-Charismatic Prophecy*, 189.

164. Muindi, *Pentecostal-Charismatic Prophecy*, 186.

This experience proceeds along a continuum. First, the prophet experiences revelatory promptings in the human conscious dimension. As the prophet submits to these promptings, there is a "decreasing intensity of human consciousness" with a corresponding "increasing intensity of ecstatic sacramental experience."[165] This leads the prophet through the "deep human unconscious dimension" into the divine presence of the Holy Spirit.[166] Muindi's research subjects described the experiences in phrases such as: "overwhelming compulsion to speak," "a sense of being physically overpowered," "a sudden rush of energy into body," "like being submerged in the Holy Spirit," and "no longer aware of earthly things."[167] Meredith McGuire observed the intense sacramental nature of the prophetic experience in her 1977 sociological study of American Roman Catholic charismatics. She found three interrelated elements regarding the social function of prophecy: "(1) an atmosphere of expectancy; (2) a sense of mystery; and (3) the immediacy of God."[168] This sense of the immediacy of God has been a fundamental element of Pentecostal worship from its earliest days and is only intensified during the prophetic experience.[169]

Muindi's context most clearly reflects this sacramental theme. Other empirical researchers have found the experience to be less intensely sacramental. While Cartledge mentions that "a number of interviewees described the pressure they feel, or have felt, prior to, or simultaneous with, the delivery of the message,"[170] many experienced the revelatory impulse in more pedestrian ways, including seeing pictures while praying, receiving knowledge about a situation ahead of time, or having Scripture verses come to mind."[171] The Church of England context of Cartledge's study accounts (at least in part) for these differences. His subjects were not always participating in a charismatic worship service when prophesying. "Prophetic experiences cannot be limited to experiences which occur in corporate worship . . . There may be no sharp line of division between experiences which occur

165. Muindi, *Pentecostal-Charismatic Prophecy*, 191.

166. Muindi, *Pentecostal-Charismatic Prophecy*, 191.

167. Muindi, *Pentecostal-Charismatic Prophecy*, 191.

168. Cartledge, *Narratives and Numbers*, 10. See also McGuire, "Social Context."

169. Samuel argues that "Pentecostal identity has been shaped by the anticipation of direct and present experiences of the Spirit—the Spirit's immediacy—in corporate worship, whereby participants in Pentecostal corporate worship might also claim that 'God is really among us'" (*Holy Spirit in Worship Music*, 1).

170. Cartledge, *Narratives and Numbers*, 20.

171. Cartledge, "Charismatic Prophecy," 79–81.

in private prayer and those which occur in corporate worship."[172] Lum's research differs from Muindi in that "70.27 percent reported that they are almost never in a trance while prophesying . . . Significantly, no respondent claimed that they always prophesied while in a trance. Furthermore, 60.13 percent of the respondents are often or almost always able to cease prophesying at will."[173] This divergence could reflect regional differences in prophetic experience: perhaps Kenyan prophets are more ecstatic practitioners than Singaporean prophets. The language "trance," however, could have been interpreted pejoratively by Lum's subjects. One can only wonder how Lum's subjects would respond to Muindi's more nuanced explanations of the intense sacramental experience. Harris reports, on the basis of ethnographic studies of three congregation, that "while all three churches in the study placed value on the hearing God experience, expression of this varied significantly."[174] Churches that make the facilitation of revelatory experiences a high priority lead to "high-level experiences."[175]

Muindi's sacramental-experiential model of CP coheres with the experience of the Old Testament prophets. Consider Saul's experience with the band of prophets "in a prophetic frenzy." The spirit of the Lord rushed upon Saul, he prophesied with the band, and as a result, was turned "into a different person" (1 Sam 10:5, 6). Ezekiel experienced the presence of God with such weight that he "fell on his face" (Ezek 1:28) only to be lifted back to his feet by the command of God and empowerment of the Spirit (Ezek 2:1–2). Even the final product of the literary prophets need not exclude such experience. Strawn and Strawn note that behind the various prophetic literary forms such as the call narrative and prophetic lawsuit "there is a life experience or event (*Sitz im Leben*) behind the literary form."[176] This life experience may well include "trance behaviour"[177] or "stereotypical prophetic possession behaviour."[178] By way of contrast, the less trance-like experience reported by Cartledge, Lum, and Harris suggest an area of discontinuity.

---

172. Cartledge, "Charismatic Prophecy: A Definition," 83.

173. Lum, *Practice of Prophecy*, 184.

174. Harris, "The Wacky, the Frightening, and the Spectacular," 205.

175. Harris, "The Wacky, the Frightening, and the Spectacular," 200. "High-level experiences" refers to Glock and Stark's taxonomy (*Religion and Society in* Tension, 56–58).

176. Strawn and Strawn, "Prophecy and Psychology," 616.

177. Strawn and Strawn, "Prophecy and Psychology," 616.

178. Wilson, "Prophecy and Ecstasy," 329.

Empirical Studies: Conclusion

Empirical studies on CP demonstrate a significant level of coherence between the Old Testament prophets and modern practitioners. These studies have undermined the common belief that CP serves an exclusively encouraging function, allowing the experience to resonate more closely with Old Testament prophetic warnings. Like the Old Testament prophets, people who exercise the gift of prophecy today receive that prophetic impulse in a variety of modes. The sacramental nature of prophetic inspiration is less clear on the question of coherence, with Kenyan practitioners experiencing the pathos of God more regularly than their Singaporean, British, and Australian counterparts. The experience of the Kenyans coheres more with the Old Testament prophets than those in the other studies. This diversity of expression challenges the hypothesis that the experience of modern-day charismatic prophets coheres with the Old Testament prophets since it appears that the hypothesis only faithfully describes the Kenyan experience. This study will add Canadian data to these results which will clarify the global picture.

Conclusion

There are some challenges relating the theoretical and empirical literature. While both bodies of work consider the Old Testament prophets, the theoretical literature focuses on New Testament prophecy and applies what is learned to modern CP, while the empirical literature focuses directly on modern CP. For Pentecostals (as mentioned above), CP is viewed as synonymous with New Testament prophecy, although certainly not all the writers would agree with this view. As a result, the empirical literature shows a greater level of coherence between Old Testament prophecy and CP than the theoretical literature. In sum, the empirical literature finds continuity in the practice of condemnatory prophecy where some of the theoretical writers dismiss its applicability due to a perceived conflict with 1 Cor 14:3. The empirical literature also finds continuity in the diverse ways that people receive the prophetic impulse and are drawn into an intense embodied experience with the divine during prophecy. The theoretical literature highlights discontinuity most strongly in emphasizing the relative lack of authority New Testament prophecy carries. The theoretical discussion about the break or shift in prophecy in the intertestamental times and its ultimate restoration in Jesus generally emphasizes discontinuity, although an understanding of Jesus as the point at which the Old Testament prophetic themes find their fulfillment before being transferred to the early church allows for coherence.

This conclusion raises a problem. The empirical literature is published in scholarly works inaccessible to many Pentecostal leaders whereas the theoretical works are often popularized. This means that Pentecostal praxis is informed by an incomplete view of the situation. This literature review has demonstrated that although the empirical literature more closely confirms the coherence between Old Testament prophecy and CP, this question has not been addressed directly. The phenomenological research study of chapter 4 aims to be a modest contribution to the existing body of empirical research, broadening the cultural setting under investigation by including Canadians from the PAOC and PAONL.

Chapter 3: The Prophetic Experience of the Hebrew Prophets

THE PHENOMENON OF PROPHECY in the Old Testament is massive both in scope and significance.[1] The data is wide-ranging, with prophecy appearing throughout the Hebrew Bible in the Torah, the narratives of the Former Prophets, and the prophetic anthologies of the Latter Prophets, both pre- and postexilic.[2] Brueggemann divides the prophetic phenomenon of prophecy into two parts: "*individual persons* and . . . a *literary corpus*."[3] The concern of this chapter is to identify the experience of *individual persons* as mediated through their extant *literary corpus*.[4] To do so, this study will narrow its focus to the experience of the prophet Jeremiah. Jeremiah is an obvious choice of subject because, as Timothy Polk observed:

> Nothing distinguishes the book of Jeremiah from earlier works of prophecy quite so much as the attention it devotes to the person of the prophet and the prominence it accords to the prophetic "I", and few things receive more scholarly comment. The introductions typically observe that we learn more of Jeremiah's life and

1. Brueggemann writes: "The general phenomenon of prophecy in Israel is enormously diverse in its many manifestations. Any generalization about prophecy is likely to fail to comprehend the data" (*Theology of the Old Testament*, 622).

2. While the Torah "contains no prophets in the technical sense of the term" (Schmitt, "Preexilic Hebrew Prophecy," 482), this does not mean that prophecy did not exist. Indeed, Moses came to be viewed as the paradigmatic prophet. "Whatever else Moses is and does, his prophecy, his ministry of the word, is the crystal center of his nature and work . . . He represents the Lord, he enunciates the message, and commands in His name" (Buber, *Prophetic Faith*, 71). For a Pentecostal perspective on the Former Prophets, see Wadholm, *Theology of the Spirit*.

3. Brueggemann, *Theology of the Old Testament*, 622.

4. Shead concisely points out regarding Jeremiah, that "we have no way back to the actual experience of the prophet other than through his book" (*Mouth Full of Fire*, 254).

> personality than of any other prophet's, thanks to the abundance
> of both third and first-person materials.[5]

For this reason, Jeremiah is the ideal prophetic subject for this project. It is Jeremiah's life—his *experience*—that will be brought into dialogue with the experience of modern charismatic prophets in chapter 5. To facilitate this dialogue, this chapter will first provide a brief contextual overview of the book of Jeremiah before exploring his prophetic experience.

The five textural components of the phenomenological study will be used as a framework for exploring the experience of Jeremiah.[6] These components are as follows:

1. The prophet *recognizes* the presence of God.

2. The prophet *receives* the prophetic impulse.

3. The prophet *discerns* the source and recipient of the message.

4. The prophet *releases* the prophetic message.

5. The prophet *experiences* attendant physical and emotional sensations.

The first two textural elements—the prophet *recognizes* the presence of God and *receives* the prophetic impulse—are indistinguishable in Jeremiah's experience and will thus be combined in this chapter.

The Context of Jeremiah

Before surveying Jeremiah's experience according to the five textural components of the prophetic experience, it will be helpful to provide a brief word on the canonical, historical, and theological setting and themes of Jeremiah. As described in chapter 1, this study will take a canonical-literary approach to Jeremiah. While some basic historical-critical issues such as the date and location of Jeremiah's ministry are necessary to understand the book, the text will be taken in its final canonical form.[7]

---

5. Polk, *Prophetic Persona*, 7. See also Smith: "Unlike any other prophetic work, the book of Jeremiah concentrates dramatically on the figure of the prophet himself" (*Laments of Jeremiah*, 1).

6. These five phenomenological components are described in detail in the following chapter. The textural components were chosen to provide structure to this study of Jeremiah in order to more clearly highlight areas of continuity or discontinuity between the Old Testament Prophets and modern charismatic prophets.

7. Discerning the final canonical form of the text is a particular challenge for Jeremiah

One significant canonical feature to note is the literary relationship between the books of Jeremiah and Deuteronomy. In Deuteronomy, Moses predicted that "the LORD your God will raise up for you a prophet like me from among your own people; you shall heed such a prophet" (Deut 18:15). Benedetta Rossi argues that the book of Jeremiah presents Jeremiah himself as this prophet.[8] Indeed, the book of Deuteronomy is the largest influence in Jeremiah's life.[9] Many connections have been drawn between the books of Jeremiah and Deuteronomy, but the most significant overarching category that connects the two books is covenantal theology. Thompson writes: "Even a cursory reading of the book of Jeremiah will indicate its deep interest in the covenant between Yahweh and Israel."[10] The Mosaic covenant was "fundamental" to Jeremiah's perspective.[11] For Jeremiah, Jerusalem would fall because the inhabitants had broken the covenant and were now reaping the consequences of breaking faith (Jer 11:1–17; cf. Deut 28:15–68). Jeremiah's use of the Deuteronomic tradition will be significant later when we explore the way in which Jeremiah and modern-day charismatic prophets value Scripture.

Historically speaking, the ministry of Jeremiah is explicitly dated from the thirteenth year of King Josiah's reign until the captivity of Jerusalem,

---

since the MT and LXX order the text in different ways. Rosenberg writes: "The structure of Jeremiah, and especially of its apparently chaotic chronology, has proven elusive to critical investigators, many of whom have declared the text to be in disarray and have attempted a reconstruction of an 'original'" ("Jeremiah and Ezekiel," 190). Beal writes that there are at least three different approaches to structuring book. This study will pay particular attention to the internal disjunctive headings noted by Shead (*Mouth Full of Fire*, 62–106).

8. Rossi, "Reshaping Jeremiah," 575. Jeremiah was not the only prophet to be viewed in this light. We have already seen in the literature review how Jesus is presented by Luke as the ultimate fulfillment of the prophet like Moses (Stronstad, *Prophethood of All Believers*, 44).

9. As Lundbom says, "It is clear that so far as Jeremiah's own self-understanding was concerned, the prophet looming largest for him was Moses" (*Jeremiah: Prophet Like Moses*, 3). This understanding is followed by Holladay ("Background of Jeremiah's Self-Understanding"). Others such as Seitz argue that the connections between Jeremiah and Deuteronomy are not rooted in the historical prophet's self-understanding but rather the process of redaction as future editors cast Jeremiah in this light (Seitz, "Prophet like Moses"). As stated in chapter 1, the canonical-literary approach adopted in this study renders this a moot distinction. Regardless of whether or not the historical Jeremiah viewed himself through a Deuteronomic lens, the final form of the text presents Jeremiah this way.

10. Thompson, *Book of Jeremiah*, 59.

11. Thompson, *Book of Jeremiah*, 61.

from 624–586 BC (Jer 1:1–3).[12] This time covers the downward spiritual and political trajectory of Jerusalem from the heights of the reformer Josiah and the fall of Assyria through a time of idolatrous political vacillation between Egypt and Babylon until the final destruction of the city and temple. The spiritual state of Judah during this time frame fuels Jeremiah's twofold message: judgment and hope, defeat and restoration, summarized in the words of Yahweh during Jeremiah's call:

> See, today I appoint you over nations and over kingdoms,
> to pluck up and to pull down,
> to destroy and to overthrow,
> to build and to plant. (Jer 1:10)

Jeremiah offers both messages of judgment as well as messages of hope. Israel's faithlessness will lead to destruction, but there is hope on the other side of judgment.

Brueggemann identifies features of the theological tradition of Jeremiah that explain the rationale for the messages of judgment and hope.[13] First is the Sinai tradition along with the covenant blessings and curses described by the Deuteronomist. Israel broke the covenant and trusted in other nations for their security, namely, Egyptian and Babylonian power. This is the theological rationale for the destruction of the royal city and exile from the land God promised to the patriarchs.[14] If this was the only theological tradition behind Jeremiah, the story would be dismal indeed. The second tradition and the reason for messages of hope lie in the "*pathos of Yahweh*."[15] This was popularized by Abraham Heschel, who writes: "To the prophets, sin is not an ultimate, irreducible or independent condition, but rather a disturbance in the relationship between God and man [*sic*]; it is an adverb and not a noun, a condition that can be surmounted by man's return and God's forgiveness."[16] God never finally abandons the community that breaks his covenant. This twofold movement of death and hope is embedded in the first and last chapters of Jeremiah, chapters

---

12. Allen, "Jeremiah: Book of," 424.

13. Brueggemann, *Jeremiah*, 3–6.

14. Brueggemann, *Jeremiah*, 3–4.

15. Brueggemann, *Jeremiah*, 5.

16. Heschel, *Prophets*, 295. Schlimm notes that Fretheim and Brueggemann have both taken Heschel's articulation of God's pathos and continued working on this theme ("Different Perspectives on Divine Pathos," 673). See Fretheim, *Suffering of God*, and Brueggemann, *Theology of the Old Testament*.

that function as a prologue and epilogue for the book (Jer 1, 52).[17] These two themes—the consequences of breaking the covenant and the pathos of Yahweh—are factors that directly influence Jeremiah's prophetic experience.[18] It is within this theological milieu that Jeremiah, along with his scribe Baruch, delivered the word of the Lord.

Jeremiah *Recognizes* the Presence of God and *Receives* the Prophetic Impulse

This section will consider how Jeremiah recognized and received the prophetic impulse in three ways. First, the significance of the divine word in the book of Jeremiah will be explored. Second, the prophetic call narrative will be examined. Third, the times when Jeremiah receives God's word by way of an inanimate object will be considered. As noted above, the first two textural elements of the phenomenological study are combined to create this section.[19] The implications of this will be explored further in chapters 4 and 5.

For Jeremiah, the experience of the prophetic impulse revolved around the commanding word of God, the determinative factor in his prophetic ministry. The first verses of Jeremiah set the tone: "The *words* of Jeremiah . . . to whom the *word* of the LORD came" (Jer 1:1–2, emphasis added). This book contains the word of God (singular) in the words of Jeremiah (plural). Brueggemann articulates the significance of this well when he writes that Jeremiah "is a man to whom a persistent, inescapable, and overriding word has been delivered. His life consists in coming to terms with that word, finding ways to articulate it to his contemporaries, and living with the hazardous consequences of that reality."[20] This emphasis on the divine word continues prominently throughout the book. Andrew G. Shead notes three significant

17. Allen, "Jeremiah: Book of," 423.

18. Brueggemann identified a third theme: *"royal-temple ideology of Jerusalem"* (Brueggemann, *Jeremiah*, 6). While significant for Brueggemann's interpretation of Jeremiah, this theme does not bear directly on the prophetic experience of Jeremiah explored in this chapter.

19. In modern CP, prophets often (but not always) *recognize* the presence of God before *receiving* the prophetic impulse. In Jeremiah's experience, what modern charismatic prophets regularly experience as two invariable components appear to occur simultaneously. That is, there is no clear recorded episode of Jeremiah *recognizing* the presence of God without a simultaneous *reception* of the impulse to prophesy.

20. Brueggemann, "Book of Jeremiah," 132.

features of word language in Jeremiah. First, "the vocabulary of word and words is used more liberally in Jeremiah than in any other major Old Testament book."[21] Prophetic books contain the highest percentage of speech directly attributed to God and Jeremiah leads the way in the prophetic corpus.[22] Second, word language serves as formulas that give formal structure to the book. Specifically, they include the messenger formula found 155 times in Jeremiah (e.g., "Thus says the LORD"), the narrative formula found 23 times in Jeremiah (e.g., "The word of the LORD came to Jeremiah, saying,") and the disjunctive heading (e.g., "the word that came to Jeremiah from the LORD").[23] Disjunctive headings are not proper sentences but phrases that serve as a demarcation points in the book. Third, the expression "declares the LORD," while having no structural significance, is used 167 times in Jeremiah (60 percent of all cases in the Old Testament).[24] This frequent use of word-language used in various ways underscores the significance of God's word in the prophetic experience of Jeremiah.[25]

The significance of word language in Jeremiah can be further highlighted in comparison with his prophetic contemporary. Ezekiel spoke frequently of the Spirit as the source of his inspiration. The Spirit entered Ezekiel and empowered him to stand (Ezek 2:2), lifted him up and carried him (Ezek 3:14), and entered him and spoke to him (Ezek 3:24). This contrast between Jeremiah's word emphasis and Ezekiel's Spirit emphasis is clearly seen in their complementary visions of the new covenant (Jer 31:31–34; Ezek 36:24–28). In Ezekiel's vision, God will give his people a new spirit, placing it within them. Jeremiah's new covenant has no mention of the Spirit. Instead, God will put his law (*torah*) within them, writing it on their hearts. Unlike Ezekiel, Jeremiah "has no theology of the spirit."[26]

21. Shead, *Mouth Full of Fire*, 44.

22. Lamb, "Word of God," 860.

23. Shead, *Mouth Full of Fire*, 45.

24. Statistics are from Shead, *Mouth Full of Fire*, 45–46.

25. Shead, *Mouth Full of Fire*, 45. Shead emphasizes the significance of "word" language in Jeremiah in order to make the case that Jeremiah is the best foundation upon which to build a theology of the word.

26. Shead, *Mouth Full of Fire*, 266. Shead summarizes his comments on the conspicuous absence of spirit language in Jeremiah by claiming that the spirit "is effectively represented in word language" (269). Andrew Davies more carefully nuances this idea by claiming that although word language predominates, spirit-language is not completely absent, with *ruach* occurring 18 times in 17 verses in Jeremiah (Davies, "Jeremiah," 110). These occurrences do not refer directly to the deity, although there may be "oblique and tangential references" (Davis, "Jeremiah," 128) to the Spirit through the use of "double

Rather, where you would expect to find spirit language, it is replaced with word language. Throughout the book of Jeremiah, "spirit-shaped absences" leave room for a heightened recognition of the word of God.[27]

Jeremiah's reception of the divine word was expressed differently than other prophets. Isaiah willingly volunteers to be sent with the divine message (Isa 6:8), Jonah rebels against the word (Jon 1:3; 4:2), and Amos convinces God to change his mind—twice (Amos 7:1–6).[28] By way of contrast, Jeremiah "apparently submits to the inevitable."[29] The word of God is too powerful to ignore, leaving him "shattered":[30]

> My heart is crushed within me,
>   all my bones shake;
> I have become like a drunkard,
>   like one overcome by wine,
> because of the LORD
>   and because of his holy words. (Jer 23:9)[31]

While this verse speaks to the attendant physical and emotional sensations associated with prophesying that will be explored further below, it is cited here to emphasize the way Jeremiah received the prophetic impulse: it was an overwhelming word that left the prophet "undone."[32] The divine word could not be ignored—it arrived with such a sense of urgency that it had to be released (Jer 20:9).

The power of the divine word is underscored by metaphor. Twice in Jeremiah, the word is compared to fire. Jeremiah 23:29 reads, "Is not my word like fire, says the LORD, and like a hammer that breaks a rock in pieces?" While Jer 20:9 reads:

> If I say, "I will not mention him,
>   or speak any more in his name,"
> then within me there is something like a burning fire

---

entendre" (Davies, "Jeremiah," 123).

27. Shead, *Mouth Full of Fire*, 267.

28. For a phenomenological perspective on Isaiah's religious experience, see Grey, "Reading Isaiah 6."

29. Lamb, "Word of God," 867.

30. Thompson, *Jeremiah*, 493.

31. This is one of the rare exceptions in Jeremiah where the word of God is described in the plural.

32. Miller, *Jeremiah*, 750.

> shut up in my bones;
> I am weary with holding it in,
> and I cannot. (Jer 20:9)

This metaphor provides a "bridge" between the divine realm and the natural world, enabling the reader to conceptualize the prophet's experience.[33] While there are different ways the metaphor could be understood (e.g., destroying, purifying), Wilhelm J. Wessels argues on the basis of an exegetical study that "the metaphor of fire is functionally applied to give expression to the power of YHWH's word."[34] This powerful fiery word that marked Jeremiah's prophetic ministry was first received in his boyhood as indicated in the call narrative (Jer 1:4–19).

"Call narrative" indicates a literary genre where the prophet is called by God and commissioned to the prophetic task.[35] In Jeremiah's call narrative, the Lord announced Jeremiah's divine calling, Jeremiah resisted, then "the LORD put out his hand and touched my mouth; and the LORD said to me, 'Now I have put my words in your mouth'" (Jer 1:9).[36] In this act, the Lord negates Jeremiah's earlier protest that he is too young and does not know how to speak (Jer 1:6).[37] The prophet's personal qualifications are irrelevant because "the prophet is a vessel of the divine word."[38] With God's words in his mouth, his prophetic mission will be efficacious because God watches over his word (Jer 1:11). Jeremiah, perhaps due in part to his inexperience, cannot resist the overwhelming power of the divine word.[39]

Oddly enough, nowhere in Jeremiah is the prophet said to have "heard" God's words.[40] Rather, the word (singular) of God always comes to Jeremiah. The emphasis is not placed on the prophet's ability to hear but on God's ability to speak. God's words are placed in Jeremiah's mouth by the

---

33. Wessels, "My Word Is Like Fire," 501.

34. Wessels, "My Word Is Like Fire," 494.

35. Phinney, "Call/Commission Narratives."

36. This verse is a literary echo of Deut 18:18, identifying Jeremiah as a successor to Moses (Thompson, *Jeremiah*, 149).

37. This reticence to speak is a common feature in prophetic call narratives. Cf. Moses' reluctance to speak because of his lack of eloquence in Exod 4:10. Phinney observes that Jeremiah's commissioning was more similar to Moses' than any other prophet ("Call/Commission Narratives," 66).

38. Miller, *Jeremiah*, 581.

39. Miller, *Jeremiah*, 582.

40. Shead, *Mouth Full of Fire*, 55.

hand of God. This metaphor is extended later in Jeremiah where the word of God in his mouth is ingested like food:

> Your words were found, and I ate them,
>> and your words became to me a joy
>> and the delight of my heart;
> for I am called by your name,
>> O Lord, God of hosts. (Jer 15:16)[41]

Patrick D. Miller notes that the purpose of this metaphor is to connote "Jeremiah's appropriation of the words of the Lord," with the expression "called by your name" serving as a legal statement denoting divine ownership.[42] Shead also recognizes how Jeremiah appropriates God's word, placing them in his own words. At times, the initial word of God is modified by Jeremiah. "Situations where the originally given words are reshaped are not uncommon."[43] Despite this, the word is no less of divine origin. The metaphor implies that as the prophet digests God's word the message becomes part of him, able to be freely expressed in different human words. "He eats God's words, they enter his bloodstream and his bones; and when he opens his mouth, God's words come out—not because God forces him to speak them, but because there is nothing else in him to come out."[44]

Occasionally God uses physical objects in a symbolic manner to speak to Jeremiah and through which to communicate the prophetic message. There are four times in the book of Jeremiah when the prophet sees a physical item and offers a prophetic interpretation. Two occurrences happen during Jeremiah's call narrative. First, the Lord pointed out an almond branch and declared based on a play on words that he is "watching" over his word to perform it (Jer 1:12).[45] Next, the Lord pointed out "a boiling pot, tilted away from the north" (Jer 1:13), symbolizing judgment that would come from the north. Third, Jeremiah saw two baskets of figs, both good and bad, symbolizing the good and bad exiles (Jer 24:1–10). Fourth, the Lord instructed Jeremiah to go to the potter's house to hear his words. After Jeremiah observed the potter work for a while, the Lord explained how

---

41. Ezekiel and John also describe eating God's word (Ezek 3:1–3; Rev 10:8–10).

42. Miller, *Jeremiah*, 697–98. See also Thompson, *Jeremiah*, 396.

43. Shead, *Mouth Full of Fire*, 61.

44. Shead, *Mouth Full of Fire*, 140.

45. The play on words is based on the assonance between the Hebrew words for "almond tree" (*šāqēḏ*) and "watcher" (*šōqēḏ*) (Thompson, *Jeremiah*, 74).

Jeremiah is like clay in the potter's hand (Jer 18:1–11). These four occurrences are examples of how through "symbolic perception a physical object remains a physical object but it is interpreted by a spontaneous act of reflection into a symbol of an idea of a higher character."[46]

To conclude, for the prophet Jeremiah the experience of the prophetic impulse is wrapped up in the arrival of the divine word that was placed on his lips by God for him to ingest, appropriate, enact, and declare. Jeremiah's prophetic ministry is so associated with the word of God that the Spirit of God is rarely mentioned. Instead, the experience of the Spirit is described primarily in word-language. It is telling that although we are able to know more of Jeremiah's life than any other literary prophet, we never truly *hear* his own voice—only the word of the Lord. Shead writes: "For a book that gives such prominence to the person and works of Jeremiah, there is an irony to the fact that we hear so little of his voice. It is Jeremiah's life we see, but God's voice we hear."[47] This divine word was a powerful force that for Jeremiah became irresistible even though he regularly complained about it. However, that same forceful word, that prophetic impulse that compelled Jeremiah, would be efficacious in Jerusalem—whether in the form of judgment or hope.

Jeremiah *Discerns* the Source and Recipient of the Message

One of the chief pastoral questions surrounding the practice of CP is discernment—how do we know the message is from God?[48] Unlike what is observed in the experience of modern-day prophets, we never read about Jeremiah engaging in a discernment process to determine whether the prophetic message is truly from God. However, the important question of discernment does arise in Jeremiah when he confronts Hananiah, another prophet with an alternate message. Which prophet should the community believe? A deeper consideration of this narrative (Jer 27–28) will lay the

46. Thompson, *Jeremiah*, 75.

47. Shead, *Mouth Full of Fire*, 116.

48. Discernment in modern CP takes place in different ways. Sometimes the prophet discerns, while other times the leadership of the meeting is responsible for the discernment. Sometimes the discernment is an individual process while at other times the responsibility is corporate. Sometimes discernment is practiced to determine the source of the message, while at other times it is used to determine the timeliness of the message. This will be explored in the next chapter.

groundwork for further reflection on the experiential coherence between Jeremiah and modern-day prophets in chapter 5.

Jeremiah felt the intense pull of God's calling that began before his conception and therefore was not of his own choosing, as indicated in the call narrative:[49]

> Before I formed you in the womb I knew you,
>
> and before you were born I consecrated you;
>
> I appointed you a prophet to the nations. (Jer 1:5)

It is impossible to know how this calling impacted Jeremiah's childhood, but we do see that from a young age (Jer 1:6), he understood the powerful calling.[50] As discussed in the former section, the word of God was an overwhelming and shattering reality in Jeremiah's life. To question whether the word was of divine origin would be absurd. Jeremiah experienced God's word as an irresistible force, like a "fire" (Jer 20:9). Just prior to that famous description of God's word, Jeremiah speaks of his relationship to God in powerful terms:

> O Lord, you have enticed me,
>
> and I was enticed;
>
> you have overpowered me,
>
> and you have prevailed. (Jer 20:7)

Robert Alter notes that "the verb represented as 'enticed' could also mean 'seduced' in the sexual sense . . . The language here harbors an oblique hint of rape, as in the report of the rape of Tamar in 2 Sam 13:14."[51] Abraham Heschel translates it thus:

> O Lord, Thou hast seduced me,
>
> And I am seduced;
>
> Thou hast raped me
>
> And I am overcome.[52]

49. Jeremiah's lack of choice in this matter is indicated not only by his preconception calling but by the sequence of first-person verbs: "'I knew you'; 'I consecrated you'; 'I set you as a prophet to the nations'" (Miller, "Jeremiah," 580). In a literary sense, God is the clear subject and Jeremiah the object of the action of these verbs.

50. It is impossible to determine Jeremiah's exact age, but he was likely a youth. See Thompson: "The exact meaning of the Hebrew word is difficult to determine, but in normal usage it refers to boys and youths" (*Book of Jeremiah*, 147).

51. Alter, *Hebrew Bible*, 2:927.

52. Heschel, *The Prophets*, 144.

This harsh translation shocks modern sensibilities and others such as Mark S. Smith claim that "given the other images in the context, the sexual interpretation seems unlikely."[53] Lundbom suggests that in this lament Jeremiah alleges that "Yahweh took advantage of his youth by forcing him into submission."[54] However, even if Heschel's language is replaced by "enticed" (NRSV) or "deceived" (NIV), the strong message of the prophet being "sucked in (or suckered in)" is obvious.[55] For the purposes of this argument, when the prophetic message came to Jeremiah, it was not a meek thing to be questioned, but a seductively overpowering force. Jeremiah had no need to discern the source of the message because the God who called him from before his birth placed his words in his mouth in such a compelling way that Jeremiah had no uncertainty about the source.

Although personal discernment on Jeremiah's part was unnecessary, the issue of discernment does arise when Jeremiah confronts Hananiah. At this point in the narrative, Nebuchadnezzar has already defeated Jerusalem, despoiled the temple, and taken the first wave of exiles to Babylon along with King Jeconiah. This act of divine judgment was prophesied in Isa 39:6–7 and the Jerusalemites had reason to believe that with this prophecy had been fulfilled since the first wave of exiles had already been deported to Babylon.[56] This sets the stage for the confrontation between Jeremiah and Hananiah, with both ch. 27 and 28 set "In the beginning of the reign of King Zedekiah" (27:1; 28:1).

Jeremiah's message is devastating. Following the Lord's instructions, Jeremiah makes a yoke to wear on his neck as a prophetic sign before prophesying the same message to three groups of people—foreign nations, King Zedekiah, and the priests:

> Bring your necks under the yoke of the king of Babylon, and serve him and his people, and live. Why should you and your people die by the sword, by famine, and by pestilence, as the LORD has spoken concerning any nation that will not serve the king of Babylon? Do not listen to the words of the prophets who are telling you not to serve the king of Babylon, for they are prophesying a lie to you. I have not sent them, says the LORD, but they are prophesying falsely in my name, with the result that I

53. Smith, *Laments of Jeremiah*, 24.

54. Lundbom, *Jeremiah Up Close*, 101.

55. Miller, *Jeremiah*, 727. Miller argues the translations "enticed" and "deceived" adequately convey the "meaning and nuance" of the Hebrew language here (*Jeremiah*, 726).

56. Shead, *Mouth Full of Fire*, 164.

> will drive you out and you will perish, you and the prophets who
> are prophesying to you. (Jer 27:12–15)

This message would have crushed the spirits of people who still clung to the ideal of a Davidic monarchy or those who followed the Isaianic tradition and believed that the judgment of Isa 39 was now complete.[57] The people had to choose whether they would believe Jeremiah's word or listen to someone else. Shead makes the astute observation that "for Jeremiah at this stage the score stands as thirty-five years of prophecy, one fulfilment."[58] It is in this moment of uncertainty that Hananiah speaks his counterprophecy:

> Thus says the LORD of hosts, the God of Israel: I have broken the yoke of the king of Babylon. Within two years I will bring back to this place all the vessels of the LORD's house, which King Nebuchadnezzar of Babylon took away from this place and carried to Babylon. I will also bring back to this place King Jeconiah son of Jehoiakim of Judah, and all the exiles from Judah who went to Babylon, says the LORD, for I will break the yoke of the king of Babylon. (Jer 28:2–4)

Hananiah's prophecy was diametrically opposed to Jeremiah's earlier word. The power struggle continues as Jeremiah (ironically or perhaps sarcastically) says "Amen!" to Hananiah's prophecy (Jer 28:6). He then reminds Hananiah that the prophetic tradition that preceded them regularly spoke about war, with messages of peace being a rarity. Only when the word of "peace" is fulfilled, "then it will be known that the LORD has truly sent the prophet" (Jer 28:9). Hananiah responds with a prophetic act of his own. Jeremiah's prophetic act was to fashion and wear a yoke around his neck to symbolize submission to the king of Babylon. Hananiah takes and breaks the yoke to underscore his prophecy (Jer 28:10–11). This theatre was witnessed by all. At a later time (the duration is not indicated), the Lord sent Jeremiah to declare judgment against Hananiah. "Listen, Hananiah, the LORD has not sent you, and you made this people trust in a lie. Therefore thus says the LORD: I am going to send you off the face of the earth. Within this year you will be dead, because you have spoken rebellion against the LORD" (Jer 28:17). The wordplay here is rich: because the Lord did not *send* Hananiah with a message of peace (but he went anyway), the Lord would *send* him off the earth.

---

57. Brueggemann, *Commentary on Jeremiah*, 251.

58. Shead, *Mouth Full of Fire*, 173.

Four conclusions can be drawn regarding the question of discernment in the confrontation between Jeremiah and Hananiah. First, both Jeremiah and Hananiah were theologically correct in their statements. Hananiah was biblically grounded in the prophecy of Isa 39 and the promise of Davidic lineage. Jeremiah's word was biblically based on the covenant curses of Deuteronomy, a major influence throughout the book. Thomas W. Overholt emphasizes this: "The curious thing is that considered apart from its historical context, there is nothing particularly 'false' about Hananiah's message . . . In [prophesying this way] he stood firmly within the tradition of the prophet Isaiah."[59] The audience was faced with a decision with no clear biblical answer. Second, neither prophet's message could be verified. Hananiah declared that within two years, the Lord would destroy Babylon's rule. With the benefit of hindsight, we see that a decade later Babylon returned to Jerusalem to besiege it again. Neither prophecy had time to be historically verified because God issued judgment against Hananiah who died within the year.[60] This leaves the criterion of fulfillment useless. Jeremiah called the people to submit to Babylon's rule *immediately*. They did not have time to wait to see whether Hananiah's counterprophecy would be verified in two years. Third, Jeremiah appeals to the prophetic tradition that preceded him: "The prophets who preceded you and me from ancient times prophesied war, famine, and pestilence against many countries and great kingdoms" (Jer 28:8). His point was that he stood in firm historical tradition when he issued judgment against Jerusalem for breaking the covenant. This does not mean that positive prophesies should always be ignored—Jeremiah himself took time "to build and plant" as well as "to pluck up and to pull down" (Jer 1:5). However, the weight of the tradition did favour Jeremiah. Fourth, this leaves the people with a choice to make with no empirical or clear conclusions to draw. "There is no test by which one can invariably and publicly verify that what one hears are the words of God, yet one is held responsible for putting one's trust in them if they are

59. Overholt, "Jeremiah 27–29," 244–45. Overholt proceeds to claim that Isaiah was convinced that Zion would never fall. Overholt cites texts including Isa 31:4–5 and 33:17–22 to support this claim. This is likely an overstatement since these texts could be considered fulfilled when the Assyrian threat was removed (Oswalt, *Book of Isaiah Chapters 1–39*, 603). However, prophetic messages that refer to Zion as an "immovable tent . . . whose stakes will never be pulled up" (Isa 33:20) could be used to support Hananiah's claim.

60. The first wave of exiles (just preceding the encounter between Jeremiah and Hananiah) took place in 597 BC. Two more waves of forced migrants left Jerusalem for Babylon in 587 and 582 BC (Ahn, "Exile," 196).

and rejecting them if they are not."[61] Jeremiah allows for no easy formulas or ways to discern which prophet to trust.

Jeremiah *Releases* the Prophetic Message

After experiencing the overwhelming immediacy of God's word, a word too strong to ignore, all that is left for the prophet to do is to release the message. Jeremiah releases the prophetic message in two primary ways: speech and sign-acts—both of which were then written and shaped into the book of Jeremiah. This section will explore Jeremiah's prophetic delivery, noting how the prophetic word often demands an obedience that runs counter to the social norms of society. Jeremiah's commitment to the divine word led to many moments of awkward obedience.

To state the obvious, we have no access to the original prophetic words Jeremiah uttered. Instead, we have a carefully curated book that contains his prophecy in a variety of literary genres, including oracles of disaster, disputations, proclamations of salvation, visions, dirges, and laments.[62] The process that created the final form of Jeremiah was characterized by "writing and rewriting, . . . not stopping until the final form of the book was fixed within the Jewish canon."[63] While the diverse perspectives and reconstructions offered by modern interpreters are beyond the purview of this project, it is worth noting that Jeremiah did have a hand in the writing of his prophetic messages with his scribe, Baruch, whom many scholars believe was responsible for much of the book of Jeremiah.[64] In Jer 36, Baruch records the prophet's dictation before reading the scroll aloud at least two

61. Shead, *Mouth Full of Fire*, 173. The need for the audience to discern the veracity of the prophetic word is amplified by a literary technique in Jer 28:5. Moore notes that after Hananiah's opening message to Jeremiah, "first-person narration abruptly gives way to third-person narration (v. 5)" (Moore, *Spirit of the Old Testament*, 93). This literary effect moves the reader from Jeremiah's side to the audience who is expected to discern the truth of Hananiah's message. While readers know from the outset that Jeremiah is right and Hananiah is wrong, the narrative forces the reader to "reconsider what was available 'in the presence of the people' and 'in the hearing of all the people' in the last days of Judah" (96).

62. Allen, "Jeremiah: Book of," 426–32.

63. Shead, *Mouth Full of Fire*, 47.

64. For a history of the interpretation of Jeremiah, see Dearman, "Jeremiah: History of Interpretation." For the role of Baruch, see Lundbom, "Baruch." Scholars who attribute the bulk of the book of Jeremiah to Baruch include Muilenburg, Gevaryahu, and Lundbom (Lundbom, "Baruch," 617).

times, first to the general public (Jer 36:9–10) and second to King Jehoiakim's officials (Jer 36:11–19). This second reading earned Baruch and Jeremiah a warning: hide before the king hears these words. King Jehoiakim
was not pleased by the scroll, carefully cutting off the words as they were
read to them and tossing them into the fire (Jer 36:20–26). After the scroll
was burned, "the word of the LORD came to Jeremiah" (Jer 36:27) instruct-
ing him to write all the words from the first scroll along with the addition
of "many similar words" (Jer 36:32).

Since it is clear there was a written component to Jeremiah's prophetic
ministry and Baruch's scribal contributions from the start, it is possible to
glimpse the way Jeremiah released the prophetic word by exploring some
of the literary features of the written text. Shead highlights three specific
literary techniques, all of which are intended to bring later readers of the
prophetic word back "with as much directness as possible" to the original
prophetic event.[65] First, the book of Jeremiah contains embedded discourse.
That is, the text never says, "God says he wants you to repent," but rather,
"God says, 'I want you to repent.'"[66] This literary feature can lead to confusing
passages such as Jer 27:5, where we read "Jeremiah quoting the LORD quoting Jeremiah quoting the LORD quoting himself!"[67] Although the nestled
quotations become confusing, this technique "has the effect of creating immediacy. We are there listening to Jeremiah."[68] The second literary technique
is the drift of the speaker. An example of this can be found in Jer 25:1–7,
where Jeremiah begins speaking to the people but by the end of the passage it is the Lord speaking. It is unclear where the shift occurred. However,
the effect of the technique is clear: "there is a strong theological imperative
in Jeremiah to have the reader encounter God's words directly, even if it
means that the voice of Jeremiah himself must slip into the background."[69]
The third literary technique is telescoping, where the author selects from
various events which ones to record. This, again, can lead to a confusing
narrative where the reader is unsure to whom the personal pronouns refer.[70]

---

65. Shead, *Mouth Full of Fire*, 109.

66. Shead, *Mouth Full of Fire*, 110.

67. Shead, *Mouth Full of Fire*, 111. Allen describes the content of this section as "a
series of quotations embedded inside quotations" (Allen, *Jeremiah*, 306).

68. Shead, *Mouth Full of Fire*, 111.

69. Shead, *Mouth Full of Fire*, 112.

70. Polk highlights the ambiguity in personal pronoun referents: "We have seen that
at one moment Jeremiah may speak in a voice that is purely his own (1.19b), while at the
next speak as or with the voice of the people (10.20, 23–25; 14:7–9, 19–22; 8.14–15), and

The effect of this technique, however, is worth the confusion, as it "dulls all other voices so as to make God's voice predominate."[71] To sum up, in his prophetic delivery (as evidenced through his written words), Jeremiah is ultimately concerned with making the word of God as clear and immediate as possible to his audience, whether to the residents of Judah or those who would read his scrolls in the generations to come.

In addition to Jeremiah's prophetic speech that was recorded by Baruch, he also performed sign-acts. These "visible words" have a long history in the Hebrew prophetic tradition and can be defined as "nonverbal actions and objects intentionally employed by the prophets so that message content was communicated through them to the audiences."[72] A brief sampling will demonstrate how pervasive this form of prophecy was. Zedekiah ben Chenaanah made horns of iron to present to King Ahab in the ninth century (1 Kgs 22:11), Isaiah went naked and barefoot in the eighth century (Isa 20:1–6), Ezekiel cooked starvation rations over dung with the Babylonian exiles, while Jeremiah ministered in Jerusalem (Ezek 4:9–15), and Zechariah made a crown for Joshua after the exile was complete (Zech 6:9–15).[73] The use of prophetic sign-acts was especially prominent during the time of Jeremiah, with most scriptural examples contained in the books of Jeremiah and Ezekiel.[74] Jeremiah was adept at this form of prophetic communication, performing seven recorded sign-acts and delegating an additional task to an emissary to Babylon. We have already considered the construction of wooden yoke that Hananiah broke in a dramatic counter-act (Jer 27–28). Jeremiah also spoiled a linen sash (Jer 13:1–11), refrained from the normal social activities of marriage and funerals (Jer 16:1–9), broke a jug (Jer 19:1–13), purchased land (Jer 32:6–15), offered wine to the teetotaling Rechabites (Jer 35:1–19), buried stones in front of Judean refugees in Egypt

---

in the next speak in a voice indistinguishable from Yhwh's (14.17–18; 9.1–5)" (*Prophetic Persona*, 125).

71. Shead, *Mouth Full of Fire*, 116. This technique was noted by Adrianus van Selms in "Telescoped Discussion as a Literary Device in Jeremiah."

72. Friebel, "Sign Acts," 707. Thompson refers to sign-acts as visible words, based on the semantic understanding that "the noun *dābār* in Hebrew means 'word,' 'thing,' 'action,' 'event'" (*Jeremiah*, 71).

73. Zedekiah ben Chenaanah's sign-act was a *false* prophecy, but this does not undermine the argument that this style of prophecy (whether it would be proven true or false) had a long history in the Hebrew prophetic tradition.

74. Fribel, *Jeremiah's and Ezekiel's Sign-Acts*, 14.

(Jer 43:8–13), and delegated the sinking of a scroll full of oracles against Babylon in the Euphrates (Jer 51:59–64).[75]

Two common misunderstandings of sign-acts should be addressed. First, prophetic sign-acts had no innate power and should not be viewed as a form of "sympathetic magic."[76] The signs had no metaphysical power, nor did they trigger a divine act when performed correctly.[77] The power of these signs lay in their rhetorical force. As Friebel states,"One need not postulate any inherent efficaciousness, but rather attribute all effects of both verbal and non-verbal behavior to their employment as persuasive tools and devices designed by the prophets to elicit specific audience responses."[78] Second, there is no indication in the text that the sign-acts were performed in an ecstatic context. The unusual (and at times bizarre) behavior was a deliberate, intentional, action performed by the prophets consciously.[79]

Sign-acts are a highly effective form of rhetorical nonverbal communication. "By its very nature, nonverbal communication tends to be more intensely emotion-producing than does verbal communication."[80] Jeremiah's acts would have produced "horror, distress, anger, quizzicality and disbelief."[81] Consider the smashing of a jug (Jer 19:1–13).[82] When Jeremiah

75. Some scholars have suggested that these sign-acts were never actually performed. Rather, they are described as literary fictions, parabolic speeches, visionary experiences, or imaginations. See Friebel, *Jeremiah's and Ezekiel's Sign-Acts*, 20–34, for a survey of the arguments for and against actual performance. Friebel argues that the sign-acts of Jeremiah and Ezekiel "were really and publicly performed by the prophets as part of their prophetic ministries," and that even if they were never actually performed, the books of Jeremiah and Ezekiel intend the reader to assume they were performed (Friebel, *Jeremiah and Ezekiel's Sign-Acts*, 34).

76. Friebel, *Jeremiah's and Ezekiel's Sign-Acts*, 42.

77. The idea that sign-acts have innate power is connected to the idea that prophetic words in and of themselves have innate power. Thiselton argues this view is based on a "mistaken view of the nature of language" ("Supposed Power of Words," 299).

78. Friebel, *Jeremiah's and Ezekiel's Sign-Acts*, 46.

79. Thompson notes that while this particular sign was unusual, the general enacting of prophetic signs was to be expected by the prophets. "Evidently the people of Israel were used to such performances from the prophets and knew how to expect a word from Yahweh through them" (*Book of Jeremiah*, 363). See also Friebel, *Jeremiah's and Ezekiel's Sign-Acts*, 372.

80. Friebel, *Jeremiah's and Ezekiel's Sign-Acts*, 443.

81. Friebel, *Jeremiah's and Ezekiel's Sign-Acts*, 445.

82. The jug referred to a "4- to 10-inch high decanter with a narrow neck and single handle whose name was onomatopoeic of the gurgling sound its liquid contents made when poured out" (Friebel, *Jeremiah's and Ezekiel's Sign-Acts*, 116).

smashed the jug, he proclaimed, "Thus says the LORD of hosts: So will I break this people and this city, as one breaks a potter's vessel, so that it can never be mended. In Topheth they shall bury until there is no more room to bury" (Jer 19:11). Friebel explains the significance of this performance: "The decanter's ruined condition correlated with the verbally created picture of the city's architectural destruction (v. 8), and the fragments of the shattered artifact lying on the ground correlated with the verbal statements of the human destruction resulting in the bodies strewn on the ground (v. 7)."[83] Earthenware jugs could not be reassembled—destruction was final. In this a dramatic visual way, Jeremiah confirmed people's worst fears in a more emotive and effective way than words alone could communicate.

To conclude, Jeremiah released the prophetic word at times in person, and during other times through the writing of his scribe, Baruch. When his prophetic messages were written down, care was taken to ensure that the reader experienced the immediacy of the divine word. Jeremiah, like the Hebrew prophets that came centuries before and after him, also performed sign-acts that had an intense rhetorical and emotive effect on the audience. Although these sign-acts were sometimes bizarre or horrifying in nature, Jeremiah faithfully enacted these visual words.

Jeremiah *Experiences* Attendant Physical and Emotional Sensations

Jeremiah is commonly known as "the weeping prophet" (Jer 9:1), but he does more than weep. Jeremiah experiences the heart-crushing (Jer 23:9) pain of a people whose disobedience has made them the recipients of God's judgment:

> My anguish, my anguish! I writhe in pain!
> Oh, the walls of my heart!
> My heart is beating wildly;
> I cannot keep silent . . . (Jer 4:19)

The abundance of first-person language in Jeremiah is regularly used to express the emotions of Jeremiah.[84] Jeremiah wore his heart on his sleeve—or, it might be said, *God's* heart. Shead argues that Jeremiah's emotion is actually

---

83. Friebel writes: "Principal among the uses of 'I' in Jeremiah, . . . is the expression of emotion" (*Jeremiah's and Ezekiel's Sign-Acts*, 119).

84. Polk, *Prophetic Persona*, 24.

the embodied emotion of God, an idea that resonates with Heschel's idea of the divine pathos.[85] Polk uses different language to make a similar point, describing Jeremiah's life as a "metaphor" for God's word. "Through him we see into God's pathos and purpose and into the plight and destiny of the people. Jeremiah becomes the data board on which is played out the economy of judgment and salvation."[86] As the embodied expression of God's heart, his pathos, Jeremiah experiences intense emotions. A brief look at the concept of the divine pathos followed by an analysis of one of the most famous emotive texts in Jeremiah will make this experience clear.

Old Testament depictions of Yahweh are anthropopathic. God is described as someone who experiences indignation (Ps 7:11), compassion (Exod 34:6), regret (Gen 6:6), and jealousy (Exod 20:5), for example. Gary A. Heroin draws a helpful distinction here between passion and pathos. Passion is "an emotional convulsion" that renders rational action impossible.[87] By way of contrast, pathos "is an act formed with care and intention, the result of determination and decision."[88] By Heroin's definition, God is portrayed by the prophets as one who exhibits pathos, not passion. While the nature of God is unchanging, his pathos—his determined response to humanity—does change as a result of his people's loyalty or lack thereof.[89] The prophets experienced this pathos of God in a way that Heschel described as "overwhelmingly real and shatteringly present."[90] This experience of the immediacy of God was so powerful that prophets naturally experienced emotional resonance with the connection.[91] This connection between God and the prophets was described by Heschel as a connection between God's pathos and human agency. Jeremiah is an ideal

---

85. Shead, *Mouth Full of Fire*, 287; Heschel, *Prophets*, 285–98.

86. Polk, *Prophetic Persona*, 170–71.

87. Heroin, "Wrath of God," 991.

88. Heroin, "Wrath of God," 991.

89. Heroin, "Wrath of God," 994.

90. Heschel, *Prophets*, 285. While this language is more poetic than academic, it does justice to the poetic nature of the prophetic texts. Brueggemann describes the connection between God and the prophets in more precise language. The prophets are "compelled by an inexplicable force that is taken to be the summons of Yahweh" (*Theology of the Old Testament*, 623).

91. It is worth noting that Samuel describes Pentecostal identity as shaped by "direct and present experience of the Spirit—the Spirit's immediacy" (*Holy Spirit*, 1). This observation reinforces the connection between the experience of Pentecostals today and the Old Testament prophets.

test case among the prophets for this because he regularly embodies the pathos of God.

The book of Jeremiah is full of language that expresses the deep emotional experience of Jeremiah echoing the pathos of God. A closer look at one of the more famous passages in Jeremiah will highlight one of these emotions—the feeling of needing to release what cannot be held in:

> If I say, "I will not mention him,
>> or speak any more in his name,"
> Then within me there is something like a burning fire
>> shut up in my bones. (Jer 20:9)

This passage is situated in one of Jeremiah's laments or confessions.[92] These unique literary features were first noted by Duhm in 1901.[93] The six laments serve a literary purpose in "defending the legitimacy of Jeremiah's prophetic vocation in the face of resistance."[94] In addition to this, they serve three more tangential purposes: to "announce Yahweh's judgment against Israel, to show the people's fault, . . . and finally, to present Jeremiah's special identification with Yahweh as a sign and symbol of Israel's relationship with Yahweh."[95] In the sixth and final Lament (20:8–13), Jeremiah's prophetic life is recapitulated:[96] Yahweh made him a prophet, and that is the reason he is ridiculed. When he prophecies "destruction" he becomes a social outcast—even his friends look to denounce him. Jeremiah thinks about refusing to speak Yahweh's words, but he is compelled to, lest the message of judgment burn him from the inside. In the end, Jeremiah confesses that Yahweh is a strong warrior who is able to rescue the needy, including Jeremiah himself.

---

92. The six laments of Jeremiah are found in 11:18–23; 12:1–6; 15:15–21; 17:14–18; 18:19–23; 20:7–13.

93. Smith, *Laments of Jeremiah*, xiii.

94. Smith, *Laments of Jeremiah*, xx.

95. Smith, *Laments of Jeremiah*, xx. Runck argues the laments (also known as confessions) were intended as more than a description of Jeremiah's encounter with the *pathos* of God, but rather serve to "re/orient the listener's heart to mirror the heart of the prophet as heard in the outcries of the Confessions" (Runck, "Pentecostal 'Hearing,'" 255). The laments, then, are not accidental biographical insertions, but "intentional to the book's overall purpose" (Runck, "Pentecostal 'Hearing,'" 255).

96. Smith, *Laments of Jeremiah*, 24.

Jeremiah 20:9 expresses the prophet's pain. God's word is like fire, a word suggesting the theophanic presence of God that burns in judgment.[97] If the prophet speaks Yahweh's word, he is mocked. If he tries to contain the fire, literally keep it "imprisoned in [his] bones,"[98] it wearies him. Brueggemann makes poignant Jeremiah's dilemma: "When he speaks, Yahweh does not support him. When he is silent, Yahweh does not console him."[99]

Two literary features underscore the message. First, this section is "crowded with words of speaking."[100] Jeremiah is called to *speak* Yahweh's *words* that lead his enemies to *speak* of Jeremiah's demise. The verbal nature of Yahweh's message is fundamental to the prophet. Second, there is a "paranomasia involving the words *'ûkāl* and *kalkēl* in v. 9."[101] According to the MT pointing, "Jeremiah is weary with containing the world."[102] Change the vocalization and the phrase can mean, "I am tired of feeding when I do not eat."[103] "With this wordplay, the sense is that Jeremiah cannot contain the word, nor can it sustain him."[104] The following anecdotal paraphrase may sum up Jeremiah's experience in the first person:

> I felt the pressure. I knew that God wanted me to speak, but I was uneasy with the message. Surely God has better news that this! I tried to hold back, but not speaking was worse—it was almost physically painful. The situation was clearly no-win. Speak and face the suspicion of the community. Refuse to speak and face the fire of God. In the end, this was no choice—how could I imprison the fire of God in this mortal body?[105]

To conclude, Jeremiah experienced intense emotions associated with his prophetic ministry. In one sense, these emotions were his own, but in a deeper sense, Jeremiah embodied the pathos of God. "The speaker of the word is one with God. He embodies the word at the level of his being; his words are God's words, his feelings, God's feelings. His whole life is the message, embodying the judgment and promise he came

97. Levenson, "Unnoticed Connotations," 225.

98. Thompson, *Book of Jeremiah*, 460.

99. Brueggemann, *Jeremiah*, 182.

100. Smith, *Laments of Jeremiah*, 24.

101. Smith, *Laments of Jeremiah*, 25.

102. Smith, *Laments of Jeremiah*, 25.

103. Smith, *Laments of Jeremiah*, 26.

104. Smith, *Laments of Jeremiah*, 26.

105. Paraphrase developed by the author.

to announce. In him God makes himself present to his people."[106] These emotions frequently reflected the pain of rejection with accompanying tears (Jer 9:1) but also cover anger and grief. Specifically, Jer 20:9 demonstrates the powerful inevitability of the divine word—it must be released regardless of the consequences.

Conclusion

This chapter has focused on the prophet Jeremiah because as Lundbom says, "No other prophet bears his soul to the extent Jeremiah does."[107] This is not to say that Jeremiah's experience is emblematic of every other prophet. Rather, Jeremiah's experience provides the clearest opportunity to explore the potential coherence between the experience of the Hebrew prophets and modern-day prophets. This survey has demonstrated that Jeremiah *recognized* the presence of God and *received* the overwhelming prophetic impulse. While the prophet never expressly *discerns* whether the voice he hears is from God, we do see the burden of discernment placed on the audience when he challenged the false prophet Hananiah. Next, Jeremiah *released* the prophetic word in three ways: verbally, in writing through his secretary Baruch, and through the use of prophetic sign-acts that conveyed profound rhetorical force. Finally, we considered through an examination of the divine pathos how Jeremiah actually embodied the word of God, *experiencing* many attendant physical and emotional sensations. The following chapter will provide a phenomenological description of the modern-day practice of CP in the PAOC and PAONL before explicitly examining in chapter 5 how the experience of the Hebrew prophets and modern-day prophets cohere.

---

106. Shead, *Mouth Full of Fire*, 144. There is an obvious connection here between Jeremiah's embodiment of God's word and Jesus as the Incarnate Word made flesh (John 1:14). Not everyone so fully links the experience of Jeremiah with God. Lundbom highlights how in the laments, we hear Jeremiah's voice clearly: "In [the confessions], the prophet is not so much speaking Yahweh's word with power and passion, although some of this is definitely to be found in them, but rather telling us how he feels about what is going on, and what impact his preaching is having on him personally" (*Jeremiah Closer Up*, 75).

107. Lundbom, *Jeremiah Closer Up*, 75.

Chapter 4: The Prophetic Experience
of Pentecostal Prophets

THE PREVIOUS CHAPTER INVESTIGATED the prophetic experience of Jeremiah. This chapter seeks to do the same for modern-day charismatic prophets in the Canadian context. In order to accomplish this, a qualitative research study was designed and conducted using the phenomenological methodology outlined in chapter 1. The goal of this qualitative study is descriptive. It will present "a unified statement of the essences of the experience of the phenomenon as a whole"—a rich composite description of the prophetic experience as it is lived in the PAOC today.[1] Data analysis and representation will generally follow the procedure outlined by Moustakas.[2] The results of the study are presented in this chapter under four headings. First my own multifaceted experience with CP will be explored, following Moustakas's instruction to "obtain a full description of your own experience of the phenomenon."[3] Second, a brief overview of the eight research participants will be provided. Third, the process of data validation will be detailed. The bulk of the chapter will consist of the fourth section, which

1. Moustakas, *Phenomenological Research Methods*, 100.

2. *Phenomenological Research Methods*. I have shifted from Moustakas in one minor way. Moustakas advises creating individual textural and structural descriptions for *each* co-researcher (i.e., research participant) *before* developing a composite synthesis of the textural and structural descriptions (*Phenomenological Research Methods*, 182). I have followed Creswell and Poth's modification of Moustakas by developing a list of significant statements from *all* participants and grouping them into "meaning units" before developing the composite synthesis of textural and structural descriptions (Creswell and Poth, *Qualitative Inquiry*, 201). Keeping textural and structural elements distinct throughout the process allowed the unique voices of the participants to be heard more clearly as the final composite narrative was composed.

3. Moustakas, *Phenomenological Research Methods*, 122. This process attempts to "set aside the researcher's personal experiences (which cannot be done entirely) so that the focus can be directed to the participants in the study" (Creswell and Poth, *Qualitative Inquiry*, 201).

describes the experience of prophecy based on the phenomenological interviews. This section is further divided into four subsections. First, a textural description will provide "the 'what' of the appearing phenomenon."[4] Five textural components will be identified to describe the invariant essence of the phenomenon. Second, the structural description will explore "*how the phenomenon is experienced*."[5] Three structural components will be identified that influence how prophecy is experienced. Third, a brief reflection on the experience of time will clarify how the textural and structural components interact. Fourth, the textural and structural components will be woven into a composite first-person narrative.[6]

Personal Experience with CP

No researcher is unbiased as they approach their subject, a truth particularly relevant in PLR. In this section, I will present my own experience with CP in order to help bracket my own experience before analyzing the interview data. CP typically involves three agents: the prophet, the recipient, and the facilitator (often a worship leader or pastor). I have participated in all three of these roles during my pastoral ministry.

I *experience* the prophetic inspiration of God infrequently. Occasionally I have felt the Spirit urging me to contact someone or pray with them about certain topic. However, one defining event comes to mind when I clearly prophesied.[7]

> I was leading worship from a microphone—not an instrument—which was uncomfortable for me. I felt much more at home behind the reassuring bulk of a piano. Standing up with nothing but a microphone between me and the congregation left me feeling exposed. It also gave me more opportunity to actually see the worshippers without the distraction of the keyboard. The PAOC church was full with around 250 people in attendance that morning.
>
> Everyone knew me as an analytically minded teacher—not an emotional person. My natural disposition is not outgoing or demonstrative. The service this Sunday morning was dry and people were unengaged and distracted throughout the song service. I

4. Moustakas, *Phenomenological Research Methods*, 78.

5. Moustakas, *Phenomenological Research Methods*, 79.

6. For a clear summary with examples of this methodology, see Wertz et al., "Composite First Person Narrative."

7. The following account is adapted with some editorial changes from my journal.

could hardly wait to get through the final song so I could wrap up the singing and turn it over to the lead pastor. Suddenly, I felt overwhelmed and began to tear up. I experienced a sense of deep pain that I could not contain, so I stood there weeping in front of the congregation. People did not know what was happening and I certainly had never experienced anything like this before! The prophetic message from God that I managed to croak out through sobs was simply, "How do you think God feels being ignored?" This was an abbreviated translation of what I heard God speak to me. "If you think you're uncomfortable and irritated by the lack of response from the church, how do you think I feel?" The voice was inaudible but it was no less real. In that moment I believe I experienced the pain that God feels when his people ignore him.

The worship service changed in an instant. People began to repent and pray. The musicians took over since I was having difficulty speaking. God certainly made himself—his passionate heart—known to the congregation that morning.

In reflecting on that experience, there is much to analyze. First, the lack of instrument left me aware of both my own insecurity and a clear vision of the congregation's lack of responsive. Perhaps this lack of worship had occurred in previous Sundays but I did not perceive it due to the security of a piano. Second, I was caught off guard. Although I was leading the song service that requires some amount of spiritual acuity, my awkward frustration with the lack of response from the congregation left me with no experiential awareness of God's Spirit. Third, I have no way to explain the profound emotion I experienced. It arrived unexpectedly and was completely out of character for me. I tried to withhold the emotion out of embarrassment, but I could not. Fourth, the message I heard from God was more detailed and profound than I could share during the moment. However, what I did manage to share was enough that it led to the collective repentance of a large congregation. Fifth, upon post-experience reflection, I recognized that my experience mirrored the pathos of God. As I stated above, I rarely prophesy in this way. This singular event eclipses all other experiences as the definitive moment when I felt certain of God's prophetic inspiration.

I have been the *recipient* of a prophetic message many times throughout my life and ministry. I have a clear memory of attending a youth convention as a teen. A woman I did not know from the row in front of me turned during the noisy worship service and declared: "I see you on a stage in front of hundreds of people telling them about Jesus." At the time

I thought it was the confirmation of my dream to be in a contemporary Christian music band. As I entered Bible college and trained to be a pastor, I often thought back to that moment as a confirmation of God's guidance in my life. In addition to this personal word, I have received general prophetic messages as a member of various PAOC congregations many times. I would sometimes question whether these prophets were genuine or if they were just following old habits.[8]

As a pastor, I have *facilitated* the expression of charismatic gifts regularly. Sometimes I feel a sense of expectancy, often during a quiet time of worship before a prophet speaks up and encourages the congregation. On occasion, I have felt strongly that God wanted to speak to the congregation so I paused and waited in silence until someone spoke. Not every prophetic word is divinely inspired. At times, people share out of the overflow of their own devotional lives. Although I do not always feel that these messages are timely, I have regularly been surprised by members of the congregation who share later how such a message impacted them. The most difficult moments to facilitate are when someone prophesies words that I discern to be in error. At times, people with significant mental illness have spoken out of their pain and discouraged the congregation. In a small church, people are usually gracious in moments like these, and I seek to speak with the prophet later during the week to counsel them.

To conclude, I deeply value the gift of prophecy and the way the congregation experiences the immediacy of God when a legitimate prophecy is spoken. Although there are dangers associated with this gift, I believe the reward is certainly worth the uncomfortable moments. My personal experience with prophecy, especially that moment when I felt the pained heart of God during a song service, is a major reason why I have chosen to research this topic.

Research Participants

The number of research participants required for phenomenological research varies between three and twenty-five people who have experienced the same phenomenon.[9] This study involves eight subjects who practice

8. I wrote about this experience in "Sunday Morning Prophets."

9. Creswell and Poth suggest recruiting "3 to 4 individuals to 10 to 15" research participants but later note that Polkinghorne suggests "5 to 25" (*Qualitative Inquiry*, 76, 79). Moustakas, whose methodology I follow in this study, does not indicate an ideal sample

CP and who also attend a PAOC or PAONL church regularly. In order to ensure the reliability of the subjects, they were each recommended by the pastor of their church or personally hold credentials with the PAOC or PAONL. Another reason to contact potential subjects indirectly through their pastors was ethical. In this way, the subjects were able to decline without feeling any undue pressure.[10]

The eight interview participants were also chosen for their diversity. Geographically, this study includes participants from British Columbia and Yukon, Saskatchewan, Western Ontario, Eastern Ontario and Nunavut, and Maritime districts, as well as a participant from the Pentecostal Assemblies of Newfoundland and Labrador. Four of the participants were male and four were female, with ages ranging from the late twenties through the late seventies. Three of the participants were people of color. The participants represented a range of church sizes from small congregations of approximately fifty regular attendees to large churches of approximately nine hundred regular attendees. Urban and rural churches were also represented. Finally, this group of participants also includes people in a variety of leadership roles from lead and associate pastors to volunteer leaders and domestic mission workers. The diversity of situations and perspectives represented in this group of participants provided a multifaceted picture of the phenomenon.

The open-ended phenomenological interviews ranged from twenty-nine minutes through seventy-six minutes.[11] Each interview began with a broad question: "How do you experience the prophetic inspiration of God?" This question led the subject to reflect on specific moments and situations in their life where they experienced the phenomenon of CP. Through the use of prompting questions, the subject was brought back to those situations and was able to explore the experience in more detail. A list of six

---

size. Bartholomew et al. conducted a study that analyzed the effectiveness of various sample sizes in phenomenological research. They concluded that while recommending a sample size was "contrary to other theoretical positions" on phenomenological research, their findings "can be considered alongside calls for small samples," having discovered that smaller samples generally led to studies of better quality ("Choir or Cacophony?," 12). Åkerlund conducted a successful phenomenological study of Pentecostal leadership using four subjects (*Phenomenology of Pentecostal Leadership*).

10. This study was reviewed by the McMaster University Research Ethics Board and received ethics clearance.

11. The mean interview length was forty-nine minutes; the median interview length was fifty-one minutes.

further questions was in hand, but these were altered and/or dismissed depending on the ebb and flow of the interview.[12]

Data Validation

In order to ensure academic rigor, steps have been taken to validate the qualitative research that follows. Moustakas only briefly touches on the validation of phenomenological data so I have supplemented Moustakas with additional validation strategies from John W. Creswell and Cheryl N. Poth.[13] Five validation strategies have been followed. The first two strategies concern the perspective of the researcher. First, in the footnotes below, a "negative case analysis" is noted concerning moments where prophets do not experience the presence of God *before* receiving the prophetic impulse.[14] This unexpected finding directly led to the reflection on the experience of time later in this chapter. Second, I have clarified bias through "engaging in reflexivity."[15] This strategy involves writing out my own experience with CP that was done at the beginning of this chapter. One bias that was disconfirmed in the research was the notion that prophets experience the pathos of God. While emotional responses are present throughout CP, nothing in the interviews indicated that the emotions matched the tenor of the message. Third, from the perspective of the participants, I have solicited "participants' views on the credibility of the findings and interpretations."[16] This validation method, promulgated by Moustakas, was met by every participant who was willing to continue in communication after the initial

12. Moustakas describes the interview process: "The phenomenological interview involves an informal, interactive process and utilizes open-ended comments and questions. Although the primary researcher may in advance develop a series of questions aimed at evoking a comprehensive account of the person's experience of the phenomenon, these are varied, altered, or not used at all when the co-researcher shares the full story of his or her experience of the bracketed question" (Moustakas, *Phenomenological Research Methods*, 114). See also Creswell and Poth, *Qualitative Inquiry*, 79. For the list of additional research questions, see appendix 1.

13. Moustakas suggests only one validation method—input from research participants (*Phenomenological Research Methods*, 110–11). Creswell and Poth describe nine validation methods, recommending researchers use at least two of the strategies (*Qualitative Inquiry*, 259–60).

14. Creswell and Poth, *Qualitative Inquiry*, 261.

15. Creswell and Poth, *Qualitative Inquiry*, 261.

16. Creswell and Poth, *Qualitative Inquiry*, 261.

interviews.[17] The final validation strategies concern the reader. Fourth, a "rich, thick description" of the phenomenon was created through the use of many direct quotations.[18] Hearing the components of CP richly described in the participants own words enables the reader to fully engage in the phenomenological description. Fifth, a draft of this chapter was sent to an academically qualified practitioner for "peer review."[19] This academic practitioner indicated that the phenomenological description faithfully described their understanding of CP.[20] On the basis of these multiple strategies, I am convinced of the rigor and validity of the qualitative data.

Phenomenological Description

The description of the phenomenon will proceed in four sections. First, statements from the participants will be thematically arranged to create a textural description of CP. Second, a structural description will be created by examining the context and setting that influenced the prophetic moment. Third, a reflection on the experience of time will illuminate how the textural and structural components interact. Fourth, the textural and structural descriptions will be interwoven to create a rich first-person description of the event.[21] In order to maintain anonymity, research participants will be referred to as P1 through P8.

17. Five participants explicitly indicated that the findings of this phenomenological study faithfully represented their understanding of CP. The remaining three did not respond to my inquiries. This feedback was solicited in two stages. First, a draft of this chapter was emailed to the participants. This received minimal feedback, perhaps due to the length and academic nature of the writing. Second, a brief video was created to summarize the research. This video prompted a response from five of the participants.

18. Creswell and Poth, *Qualitative Inquiry*, 263.

19. Creswell and Poth, *Qualitative Inquiry*, 263.

20. The academic practitioner has decades of experience pastoring in PAOC churches and holds a DMin. This verification method led to a fruitful conversation that did not change the phenomenological description but did aid in analysis.

21. Moustakas describes these steps in chapter 5 of *Phenomenological Research Methods*, 84–201. See also Creswell and Poth who rely heavily on Moustakas (*Qualitative Inquiry*, 79–80, 201).

Textural Description of Charismatic Prophecy

The phenomenon of CP consists of five textural components that comprise its structure or essence:[22]

1. The prophet *recognizes* the presence of God.

2. The prophet *receives* the prophetic impulse.

3. The prophet *discerns* the source and recipient of the message.

4. The prophet *releases* the prophetic message.

5. The prophet *experiences* attendant physical and emotional sensations.

The following section will provide a rich description of these five textural components using the language of the research participants.

1. The Prophet Recognizes the Presence of God

Before prophets receive the prophetic impulse, they first recognize the presence of God. The subjective recognition of the divine presence can be facilitated by a variety of means, including spiritual attentiveness that is supported by the practice of personal piety, and a favorable spiritual atmosphere that includes cues from other people. However, none of these factors are viewed as prerequisites for recognizing the presence of God— sometimes prophets feel surprised by the presence of God, often in unusual circumstances.[23]

"THE CONDITION OF THE HEART—IT MATTERS" (P5)

Regardless of the setting where prophecy occurs, participants focused on one key internal condition that facilitates the prophetic moment: spiritual attentiveness. Participants describe this in various ways. P1 describes it as

22. For an elaboration of this, see Moustakas, *Phenomenological Research Methods*, 78–79, and Creswell and Poth, *Qualitative Inquiry*, 80.

23. Moustakas notes: "Texture and structure are in continual relationship." These two components "come together to create a fullness in understanding the essences of a phenomenon" (*Phenomenological Research Methods*, 79). The closeness of this relationship is especially clear in this first textural component. For clarity, this section will focus on the prophet's subjective CP recognition of the presence of God while the first structural component (below) will focus on the setting where this recognition regularly occurs. In reality, these two are intimately linked, as the final composite description will show.

being "plugged in with the Lord, . . . as far as . . . prayer time and stuff." This sense of being plugged in gives her a "confidence to believe" that God would speak prophetically through her. P5 echoes this theme of attentiveness through prayer: "If you're really praying and seeking, God's gonna speak." She also mentions fasting as a way to be attentive to the voice of God, along with maintaining an attitude of "seriousness" so that "at any time" the Lord can use her prophetically. P4 offered a memorable maxim: "I like to say that prophecy begins in the ear." When people think about prophecy, they imagine someone speaking. For P4, this is backward. The first responsibility of her prophetic ministry is to listen for the voice of the Lord. When I questioned P7 about prophesying outside of a worship context, he began to question whether he is attentive enough to the Lord in his daily life: "Maybe I'm so busy all week long that I don't— . . . If I had more time to spend with the Lord all week long, I'm sure that he would . . . speak to me in different situations." Using different language—plugged in, attentive, listening, seeking, fasting, praying—the participants viewed attentiveness to God as a key contributing factor to the prophetic moment.

"THE ATMOSPHERE WAS CHARGED WITH
FAITH AND EXPECTATION" (P1)

P4 described the intensity of the presence of the Lord memorably. "I already realized that there . . . was the presence of the Lord. Then there was *the presence of the Lord.*" This divine presence is something that then "settled upon" the worshippers. Worshippers could "feel his presence" (P8). P4 emphasizes the personal responsibility on the part of the prophet to add to this atmosphere of faith and expectation by preparing personally to hear from God. "I will say that I love pre-service prayer at our church . . . I'm asking God, 'What do you have, Lord?' 'What do you have?'" P7 echoes this sentiment: "I think that *if you're open* to the moving of God, . . . if you're open to the Spirit of the Lord at any given time that he wants [he can] use you in it."

"I'll Be Honest, Sometimes I'm Not Looking for It" (P8)[24]

Sometimes recognition of the divine presence occurs expectantly. While sometimes P8 prays and asks for the prophetic presence of God, other times God breaks in when he's "not looking for it." P4 told an amusing story about being physically and emotionally exhausted following a day of ministry. At the end of the final service, all she could think about was "pillow at the Casablanca Inn" where she was booked to spend the night. Regardless, when the pastor invited people up for prayer, she was conscripted to pray. Despite her attitude and weariness, God used her to speak prophetically to multiple people who responded to the invitation. Similarly, a worship leader was adamant to say that prophecy is "not dependent on your mood either. It's not . . . I've learned through leading worship to ignore my feelings sometimes" (P1).

2. The Prophet Receives the Prophetic Impulse

There is a difference between simply recognizing the presence of God and receiving the prophetic impulse. People who do not practice CP often recognize the presence of God, especially in prayer and worship settings. Furthermore, there are times when prophets recognize the presence of God yet are not inspired to prophesy. The prophetic impulse refers to those times when prophets experience God in a way that motivates them to speak or act prophetically. Prophets are quick to attribute prophetic motivation to God—the prophetic message cannot be generated by the will of the prophet without the perceived immediate inspiration of God. The prophetic impulse takes a variety of forms that will be surveyed below.

---

24. This section contains evidence from the interviews that runs counter to the identified textural element, that the prophet recognizes the presence of God prior to receiving the prophetic impulse. This is to be expected when investigating lived experience. Creswell and Poth note that "not all evidence will fit the pattern of a code or a theme. It is necessary to report this negative analysis, and in doing so, the researcher provides a realistic assessment of the phenomenon under investigation" (*Qualitative Inquiry*, 261). Presenting this data that runs counter to the overall theme serves as a validation strategy. Ultimately, it was this section that prompted the reflection on time to follow.

"It All Depends on What You Know the Lord's Saying —It's Not at Will" (P5)

There is both commonality and diversity in the way that people receive the prophetic impulse. Prophecy always begins with an awareness that God is present and desires to communicate with and through the prophet. In those moments, "the Holy Spirit grabs a hold of your attention and you [say], 'Okay, Lord, I need to be quiet . . . What do you want me to get or what do you want me to understand" (P7)? Participants describe this moment as an intensification of the perceived presence of God. During these times prophets say that they feel "that presence" (P7), an "overwhelming presence" (P8), an "unction" (P7), a need to allow Holy Spirit to be their "pilot and guide" (P2), their "inspiration" (P2), to "flood [their] soul" (P2). While the perceived inspiration of God always precedes a prophetic word or act, the regular practice of prophecy makes the recognition of the prophetic impulse easier. A discussion with P4 nuanced this point. She writes a biweekly prophetic email, predicated on the belief that she will experience prophetic inspiration on a regular schedule. When questioned about this she replied: "I would say the *knowing* comes a little differently—the knowing comes faster . . . I would never want to have it be prophecy on tap but it wouldn't take me much to begin to prophesy."

"It Comes Kind of Like a Revelatory Splash" (P6)

While participants all feel the prophetic impulse of God and the need to respond with obedience, the specific way they experience God's inspiration is diverse. Participants report feeling the need to read Scripture, receiving a fragment of a message, hearing God during worship, dreams, visions, special insight into a situation, and the urge to perform prophetic acts. Of these different modes, the most common way prophets receive the prophetic impulse is through Scripture. While every believer can read Scripture and hear the word of God, participants note how the Holy Spirit uses the Bible to speak directly and prophetically into the present. When P1 became a Christian, she heard "this thought in [her] mind: Acts chapter 2." As a new Christian she had never read this text but through it she experienced the baptism in the Holy Spirit. When P1 prophesies today, she still feels the need to return to Scripture: "You might get a phrase, a word of Scripture" that God intends to speak to someone through you. The experience of P8 is very similar: "You could be reading a Scripture and . . . you would be like, 'Oh, that's different. I don't remember that in that context.' And you'll run into someone later in the week, and the Lord will say, 'that's the word for them.'" For this participant, the key was in the timing. The millennia-old written word of the Bible could be brought through a prophet into a situation in the present at the necessary time. "Often times . . . I've read [the Bible] and the Lord has given me an exact word for an exact time for a person or even for me." For P2 and P4, Scripture coming to mind is the main way they prophesy. P2 describes it as Scripture coming "into [her] spirit" that is similar language to P6, who receives Scripture as "an impression on [her] heart." P4 related that most of her prophecy comes "out of my time in the word when I'm before the Lord." She takes the expression "word-based" as deeply complementary, grateful for the Sunday school teachers who taught her the Bible in her youth. Although P5 experiences dreams and visions regularly, she emphasized that "the word is always the foundation" of these experiences. P7 once received one brief phrase pointing to a passage of Scripture, "Samson went down to Delilah's house," and this, weeks later, ended up being the foundation for an extemporaneous sermon. Again, the significant element of prophesying using Scripture is not the validity of the message but the proper timing of its delivery.

Like a singer who has forgotten the lyrics only to have them return to mind line by line as the music plays, over half of the participants report receiving an impulse, a fragment, or a partial message from God that had to be acted upon before the rest of the message was clear. P1 described a time when she did not know what she was going to say until the very moment she opened her mouth to speak: "There's no premeditation." P3 was actually *surprised* by the turn one of his prophetic words took: "I didn't expect to say that." P8 reflected on the reason why God speaks to him in fragments. "This might sound silly, but I think sometimes if he gives us too much, we mess up and try to do it on our own strength." The fact that participants often do not receive the entire message before they have to speak provides opportunity to develop trust. P7 once felt the prophetic impulse lead him to call a new couple attending his church to come to the front for prayer without knowing why or what he would pray about. He simply said, "Okay, Lord, I'm gonna trust you on this."

About half of the participants were gifted musically and lead the song service in their churches. This is another way that people receive the prophetic impulse. P1 allows space for spontaneous worship when she or others in the congregation will "just kind of . . . feel it." That is, the divine impulse to prophecy. This is something that happens "quite often" as she lingers on a simple chord progression. Prophecy and worship belong together and should never be disconnected. "The prophet needs to be aware that they're constantly in that disposition of worship when they do prophesy" (P5). P6 adds that leading worship is "a very big part of [his] spirituality." During times of worship leading, he reported experiencing a "subjective awareness, . . . [of] the presence of the Lord . . . through the worship." Finally, P2 reports that "God started to give [her] songs." She would write worship music alone at home, receiving the lyrics one line at a time. When the song was completed and used in congregational worship, recipients reported being touched by God through the song.

The final ways participants experience the divine impulse to prophesy are more idiosyncratic to the individual prophets.[25] P1, P5, and P7 report receiving dreams and the necessity to interpret them. For P1, dreams are "one of the most untapped prophetic experiences." P5 has refined the process of receiving prophetic dreams. "If I get up early, very early to pray and I go back to sleep, I'll get another dream." P2 experiences prophetic pictures. "I would be by the altar worshipping God, . . . and then when people would come, I would see a picture, a whole picture . . . in my spirit and it would be identical to what they're going through." P4 describes moving pictures—visions—that she sees "almost like an old-fashioned reel rolling out." It is as if she is remembering something that has happened or will happen: "It's almost like if you said to me, 'Do you remember the day that—where you were when JKF died?' And so I would have a whole scenario unfold as if the reel was rolling." P4 describes receiving indistinct information about someone. "I am worshipping and praising God, the Holy Spirit just so powerful, and I heard in my spirit, 'pray for that guy in the blue shirt.'" The strange thing was that this was a service streamed to the internet during the Coronavirus pandemic and she had no idea who the person in the blue shirt might be. She was obedient: "I don't know where you are, but I know the Holy Spirit . . . loves you and he's talking. He's answering you." In describing this scenario, the participant began to apply theoretical categories to

---

25. While I have described the various types of prophetic impulses in order of frequency, it is important not to view this as a type of quantitative statement. During the horizontalization phase of phenomenological data analysis, "every statement initially is treated as having equal value" (Moustakas, *Phenomenological Research Methods*, 97). The frequency of the type of experience does not matter but rather, whether it is fundamental to essence of the phenomenon.

it—was this a word of knowledge or a prophecy? She quickly gave up trying to categorize it and just recognized it as the inspiration of God.

3. The Prophet Discerns the Source and Recipient of the Message

Discernment is the third textural component of CP. The process of discernment involves two distinct questions and two distinct contexts. The first question the prophet asks regards the source of the message, whether it is a legitimate message from God or comes from an evil spirit or the prophet's own imagination. The second question regards the proper recipients of the message. Should this message be given to this audience at this time? The first context is the prophet's own spirit—discernment begins personally. The second context is discernment with others, especially those in authority at the time such as a pastor. The two variables mentioned lead to four possibilities regarding discernment:

1. The prophet individually discerns the source of the message.

2. The prophet corporately discerns the source of the message.

3. The prophet individually discerns the proper recipients of the message.

4. The prophet corporately discerns the proper recipients of the message.

The phenomenological interview process has uncovered examples of all four of these modes of discernment, with none taking priority. As such, the analysis of discernment will proceed in two broad categories: personal and corporate discernment.

"I Really Wrestled It—Double Checked. I Waited Even." (P3)

The personal discernment of prophecy is a natural and immediate reaction prophets have when they receive the prophetic impulse. This section will describe the various methods participants have developed to exercise personal discernment, including reflections on the two questions of discernment: source and context. Prayer is part of every participant's personal discernment process. When unsure whether or not to deliver the message, P1 advises to "just pray into it." P2 prays "in [her] spirit," by which she means silent prayer while being attentive to God. If the prophecy is legitimate, she gets a sense that, "Okay, I'm in the Spirit now. So you've got to say what God is downloading into your spirit." The metaphor of downloading reinforces the understanding that the source of the message is in God, not the prophet. Once while praying, which is perceived as a dialogue with God, P6 "felt the Lord say that this word is not [just] for you, . . . [but] actually for . . . this community of people here." P7 framed prayer and discernment within the context of spiritual warfare. He mentioned the Holy Spirit had given him a "secret" early in his Christian life that he used to verify or "safe-check" the source of the prophetic impulse. The participant did not reveal what the secret was or how it operated.[26] However, he made it clear the secret was used as a safeguard against receiving a prophetic impulse from any evil spirit.

More idiosyncratic methods of the personal discernment of prophecy include scriptural alignment, novelty, persistence, and familiarity with the divine voice. The role of illuminated Scripture as a type of prophetic impulse was explored above. In discernment, Scripture is not received as a prophetic impulse, but used as a way to discern whether or not the message is legitimate. P4 speaks of the "plumb line of the Word" by which she is able to "judge" what she has "seen," "heard," and "sense[d]." Prophecy for her must "be in alignment with the word." P3 is regularly surprised by what the Spirit speaks through him. He has come to realize that "when you find you're saying brilliant things that you're going, 'Why, I never thought about that before!' Well, that's probably the Holy Spirit." The persistence of the prophetic impulse was noted by P3, P5, and P6. "You feel the Holy Spirit saying, 'No, I need you to do that.' And it just keeps again and again keeps troubling you. He won't let it go . . . And the Holy Spirit just keeps echoing this again and again" (P5). The "prompting won't go away" (P6). P3 describes the persistence of the prophetic impulse as a way to guard against self-indulgence. Waiting after receiving the prophetic impulse allows time for the initial thought to either fade or persist. When he would allow time to pass and "still [sense] the same things," it was a sign that the message was legitimate and not just the physiological response to "a bad lunch!" Finally, P7 and P8 emphasized how over time they have grown in their ability to know the voice of God. "I think when you have a relationship," P8 said, "you *know*, this is the person . . . you recognize their voice over other voices." P7 stated it directly: "I know you and I know your voice so I'm gonna do it."

---

26. Since this was an intensely personal spiritual matter between the research participant and the Holy Spirit, I chose not to press for more information that may have clarified this discernment process.

Ironically, P5 and P8 have both discerned the prophetic impulse to say nothing. P8 was speaking with a person who was disgruntled with the church and God in general. The participant felt an overwhelming need to respond to this person's criticisms and help him see the truth. However, in his words, "I felt the Lord very clearly say to me, 'Shut up.'" So he did. He leaned back in his chair and prayed, "God, I have nothing. Actually, what I'm going to say is probably going to tick him off more. So God, I want you to speak to him." P5 tied this message to be silent to Scripture: "If he says, 'say nothing,' I keep my mouth quiet! You know, because in the abundance of words, there's sin . . . You have to be so careful today because you don't want to give more than what the Lord is really saying." This participant reports regularly hearing more from God than she is "released" to speak.

"No Prophetic Lone Rangers" (P1)

Discernment also takes place within community. As P1 memorably stated, there are "no prophetic Lone Rangers." Participants speak about discerning their prophetic message with four different groups of people: those in authority, a friend or mentor, other prophets, and the recipients of the prophecy. Discerning with an authority figure is standard practice, especially in worship services where the prophet is not the one leading the service. P3 speaks of this perfunctorily as "part of the protocol." This gives the leader an opportunity to see whether or not there is a "peace from the Holy Spirit." P8 speaks humbly about the need to "come under leadership" by presenting the potential prophetic word to the pastor before speaking aloud to the entire congregation. The pastor in these cases often confirms: "That's exactly what's going on right now. Get up and share that," or, "That's what the Lord just spoke to me. Get up there." For this participant, it was an important sign of humility to allow the pastor to make the decision whether or not the prophetic word should be spoken in the service. P1 goes so far as to suggest that being under authority is a way to "bring out the gifts." She regularly speaks with the person in authority before sharing the prophetic message, especially "if it was something directional." There was more trepidation around sharing directional prophecy, which is why she believes it is wise to share the burden of discernment. P6 described an interesting situation where he felt the prophetic impulse in a worship setting where he was a visitor. There was no obvious authority figure in charge of this praise and worship gathering, so he went to the person standing by the sound booth and shared honestly:

> And so I came up and I said, . . . "It's my first time here . . . What . . . happens for the night or whatever?" He's like, ". . . we kind of worship like this for a while, then we'll usually have . . . a short break with . . . a short message, like a devotion or encouragement and then workshops tomorrow. But tonight we actually didn't—We don't have anybody lined up to share anything." I'm like, "Oh, well that's interesting. Because I feel like . . . I'm supposed to actually share."

After a time of consideration the informal leader of the worship night told him to proceed, despite being a stranger, and P6 shared the prophetic word. Other times, especially when the prophetic message is not being shared in a formal worship service, the participant shares the message with a close friend (P7), spouse (P1), or mentor (P8) for help in discernment. P8 relates his experience with his father, who was a spiritual mentor to him: "My dad was a good guy to confirm. He'd be, . . . praying and crying out to God and singing praises in the bathtub . . . When he got out, I'd be like, 'Dad, I just feel this.' And he could . . . really assure you. 'Yep, that's what I'm feeling too, boy.'" A personal confirmation from a trusted person encourages the prophet to feel confident in the prophetic word. P3 describes the experience of sharing with a community of prophetic-type people. In those moments he feels like he's "entering into a tradition of prophets, just like the Old Testament prophets, . . . they prophesied in community not in isolation." He feels a "joy and kinship" when he's with this prophetic community.

Authority figures, a friend or mentor, and other prophets all help to discern the message *before* it is delivered. Three participants speak about receiving confirmation about the legitimacy of their prophecy by the recipients *after* it was delivered. P4 shared one prophetic experience when she was led to sing a children's song about a dog. The recipient of that odd prophecy immediately confirmed with the participant that she was a professional dog groomer and that the song along with the message that followed confirmed things in her life she had been thinking about. P2 shared how a recipient confirmed that he "identified" with what she had said. It "resonated with his spirit." This in turn built the participant's confidence in her prophetic ability: "I felt in my heart state, I felt like, 'Okay, it's confirmed.'"

4. The Prophet Releases the Prophetic Message

Although this is the most obvious textural element of CP, participants did not often speak directly about this. Perhaps this can be viewed analogously to producing a research paper. The actual printing of the final paper is the visible part, but the bulk of the work was done by the development of the thesis, research, writing, and editing. In a similar way, by the time the prophet actually speaks or acts, the heavy lifting of recognizing the presence of God, receiving the prophetic impulse, and discerning the source and proper context of the message has been completed. All that is left for the prophet to do is to speak or act. That said, three elements of the actual prophetic delivery were highlighted in the interviews: the often awkward nature of the content and delivery of prophetic messages, the role of *glossolalia*, and prophetic acts.

"How Much Is That Doggy in the Window?" (P4)

The majority of participants reported that the prophetic message of God can lead to awkward moments that must be responded to by obedience and trust. This is perhaps best represented by P4. She described praying for a person during an altar call following a church service:

> And as I walked up I heard this song. And so I approached her and I said, "Ma'am," I said, "As I approached you, I heard this song." Oh, now she's really excited . . . She is ready. Her eyes were closed. Her hands were likely raised. She is so excited. I reached up to touch her shoulder. At which moment I thought, "Well, Holy Ghost, come on the scene" and I began to sing: "How much is that doggy in the window?" And her eyes fly open and I'm going, "Hurry up Holy Ghost!"

The text of this interview does not convey the volume and passion with which she sang that old children's song! Fortunately, the Holy Spirit allowed the prophet to interpret that song and confirm events in the recipient's life. Other awkward moments include asking her husband for a dance during the service (P1), feeling the need to tell their senior pastor a harsh passage of Scripture (P8), and declaring in a service that "there's a young married man going astray" (P7). In moments like these, participants can feel "out on a limb" (P7), "stretched," with the possibility of being misunderstood (P7), "bizarre" (P8), and "looking really stupid" (P8), and "not very comfortable"

(P7). Despite these feelings of awkwardness, participants stress the necessity of obedience and trust. "I want to be obedient to you. I want to submit to what you're saying right now to the church" (P2). P3 once received the prophetic impulse in a context where he was one of the youngest people in a room full of seasoned Christian leaders. He was also a person of color in a predominantly white setting—yet he received a "heavy message, . . . almost like a charge. Like you've lost your way." When I asked whether he was concerned about people's expectations, he replied, "Well, I don't care about that anymore. Yeah, I just . . . don't care. And this is probably true to form to the old prophets. Obedience matters to me more. So I don't care if other people reject me as long as I know that God is leading me and I'm living in obedience" (P3). P7 was in a similar situation where he felt the divine impulse leading him to call out a visiting couple in a large church during the worship service for prayer. When he fled the divine impulse, he questioned. "Now that's an odd thing to do with strangers that come to visit your assembly." Despite the awkwardness, he continued:

> I know what I know what I know when I know that the Holy Spirit is dealing with me. I know that I got to walk it through no matter where it takes me. I've got to follow it through . . . It was just obeying the Lord and what he wanted to do and following his direction. And I'm very careful that when the Lord does give me instruction that I follow it to the letter.

In general, participants viewed awkward prophetic moments as tests and opportunities to demonstrate obedience to God and faithfulness to deliver the prophetic impulse, disregarding personal social costs.

"I'm Not Sure What to Pray—So All In for Tongues" (P1)

For many of the participants, speaking in tongues with or without a subsequent interpretation is a main way they release the prophetic impulse. P4 noted how "tongues and interpretation" used to be the regular way that prophecy was practiced in Pentecostal congregations in the 1960s. This participant learned to recognize the presence of the Spirit of God by waiting for an elderly saint in her congregation to begin speaking in tongues.[27] For

---

27. Humorously, she reported being utterly surprised the first time she prophesied outside of her home church context because she experienced God without the prompt of "Gramma Peterson!"

P1 and P2, speaking in tongues is a regular part of their prayer life. When unsure about what to say, they pray in tongues that allows God to speak through them without their conscious direction. This unconscious communication regularly results in prophecy as participants who have recognized the presence of God allow God to control their speech. P5 expands on this by musing, "It's like the tongue sifts away your own logical—Not that you're not rational. Not that you're not thinking, but sometimes we babble on too much when really [it is] in our own thoughts." P5 has experienced giving a message in tongues as well as interpreting her own message that she describes as a normal experience. Why should we expect someone else to interpret? "What's the difference? You can speak in a tongue and you can get that message from the Lord as to what you just said. It's no difference."

"It Was Just an Act of Obedience" (P1)

Two of the participants reported engaging in prophetic actions in addition to their prophetic speech. P1 was in the middle of a worship service when she thought she "heard the phrase, . . . just ask him to dance." She approached her husband and asked him to dance, confirming a message he had been hearing from God for at least two weeks. "I put my guitar down and I walked over to him and he doesn't know how to slow dance. But, you know, we did the best we could, and he was so uncomfortable . . . it was just an act of obedience" (P1). P4 participates in prophetic actions with some frequency. A memorable moment came when she was repenting with a group of Christians about the historic extinction of the Beothic people. One person brought a bag of soil from a historic site that the participant speculated could have contained some of the DNA of the Beothic people. As they began to pray, one person felt the impulse to sprinkle this soil out. The participant urged her spouse to sit cross-legged on the floor, representing the Beothic people. Once he did this, P4 reports: "One of the pastors [who was praying with them] goes wild. This pastor starts swinging his hand like this, and you had a sense that there was a sword happily invisible, but he was about to take off [his (the man sitting to represent the Beothic people)], head . . . And then I go, 'Oh my God, Lord, they're going to decapitate [him]!'" This final type of prophetic inspiration is unique in that it does not require the mouth or voice of the prophet, but rather their body. In a sense, their movements become their voice.

5. *The Prophet Experiences Attendant Physical and Emotional Sensations*[28]

Physical and emotional sensations regularly accompany CP and comprise the fifth and final textural component of the phenomenon. Although described in the fifth place, these sensations can and do occur at various times throughout the prophetic process—even months later when the prophetic event is recalled and shared. The variety of sensations will be described, followed by a reflection on the more general sense of urgency that accompanies the prophet's experience.

"Fire in My Belly and . . . a Whisper in My Ear" (P3)

Emotional and even physical sensations regularly accompany prophecy. Participants report "feeling something just rising up in my belly" (P1), weeping (P1, P3), feeling "weak" and falling down (P2), feeling emotionally and physically overwhelmed (P3), a racing heartbeat (P4), feeling emotionally "impacted" (P4), "feeling . . . like fire" (P5), a sense of "love and belonging" (P6), feeling "overwhelmed" (P8), "excitement" (P8), feeling "like electricity was just going through me to my whole body," (P1), "shaking" (P1), and "goosebumps" (P1). Participants treasure these experiences, P4 actually relying on the attendant physical experience to indicate when the prophetic presence of the Spirit is near. While these sensations regularly accompany the moment of prophecy, they can also arrive later. P3, after giving a prophecy to a room full of ministry leaders, reported having to go to the side of the stage to cry and pray. He likened his event to "some black preachers who . . . after preaching these heated messages, . . . kind of shake it and cool down." Suddenly, he found himself "back to normal," the emotional and physical exhaustion that immediately followed his prophecy had disappeared. P1 reported an event where she gave a message in tongues. One week following that moment she learned that her message in tongues was actually in another language that was understood by a person attending the service. The moment she realized this, she began to shake, feeling something

---

28. I had expected to hear participants describe how their emotions echoed the heart of God conveyed in the prophetic message as per my own experience described earlier. This was not the case. Participants experienced strong emotions, but these emotions bared no resemblance to the content of the message. This demonstrates how the procedure of writing personal experience with the phenomenon clarifies bias and serves as a verification strategy.

like electricity running through her body. Even as she reported this event to me, she said, "I get the goose bumps just telling you about it." P7 felt a "powerful anointing" on him as he related a prophetic encounter to me that had happened in the past. "I feel this on me now," he said, before beginning to speak in tongues during the interview. That said, there was one outlier who experiences very little emotion when prophesying. "Honestly," P8 said, "I don't feel myself getting all that emotional and all worked up. I feel his presence and I know it's him." This participant most commonly experiences the prophetic impulse of God in his day-to-day activity, relating to God as a regular dialogue partner, his "best friend" (P8).

"You've Got to Get It Out There *Right Now*" (P8)

For some, the physical and emotional sensations that accompany the prophetic impulse carry with them a deep sense of urgency that has even led to a loss of control. P1 described one such situation:

> Our church had a little getaway. I think it was New Year's. And one of our young men who was a new Christian was sharing—he was testifying—and I was just sitting there innocently, and I started feeling something just rising up in my belly and I could not control it. And I don't like to not be in control . . . , you know? Especially in front of people. I'm an introvert. But all of a sudden, what came out of my mouth was "Go!" Like, really loud, "Go!" And that was it and people started laughing.[29] And [the young man who was sharing] didn't know what to do but it was . . . an exhortation to him, you know? Just run the race. Go! I was cheering him on. But I had no control over my mouth.

Aware that the idea of being unable to control prophetic inspiration is a point of contention among biblical scholars, I continued to encourage the participant to speak about this situation while remaining in the spirit of phenomenological investigation and not raising these theoretical issues. As she continued to speak, she informed me that this one incident was unusual and that uncontrollable prophecy "hasn't happened very often." It is worth noting that this one incident was such a dramatic moment in her life that she remembered it vividly and chose to speak about it. Once

---

29. Given the context, the laughter was not joking, but understood as "holy laughter" such as was regularly experienced at the Toronto Blessing (see Barkley, "Toronto Blessing").

this "Go!" prophecy was spoken, the attendant emotional response was twofold. First, she felt "kind of silly," a sensation explored above regarding awkward prophetic moments. Second, the sense of embarrassment was mitigated by a deep sense of release. "I had to release that," she said. While this was the only participant who shared a moment of loss-of-control, two others confirmed the sense of urgency and the need to release what God had told them to communicate. P2 describes a time when she was praising God at an altar call and she had a "sense that you've got to say this now." P8 relates how "there are times when you feel like you've got to get it out there *right now*."

Textural Description Summary

Five textural components have been described in the words of the participants. The following chart summarizes the textural description. Key verbs of the components have been used to highlight the active nature of the prophetic phenomenon.

Textural Component	Features of the Component
1. Recognize	A) Spiritual attentiveness
	B) Spiritual atmosphere
	C) Unexpected presence
2. Receive	A) Received, not generated
	B) Various modes: Scripture, fragment, hearing during song service, dreams, visions, special insight, urge for prophetic acts
3. Discern	A) Individual discernment of source and context
	B) Corporate discernment with the aid of authority figures, friends and mentors, other prophets, and recipients
4. Release	A) Awkwardness
	B) Glossolalia
	C) Prophetic acts

Textural Component	Features of the Component
5. Experience	A) Sensations
	B) Urgency

Structural Description of Charismatic Prophecy

Three structural components have been identified that influence the experience of the prophetic phenomenon:

1. The prophet's mentoring.

2. The prophet's location.

3. The prophet's response to failure.

These three components serve as the background upon which the prophetic moment occurs. Mentors train prophets to prophesy. Although some participants indicate an ongoing relationship with their mentor(s), they are more regularly spoken of in the past tense as people who have contributed at significant stages in the prophet's development. The prophet's location refers to the immediate setting where the prophecy is released. As indicated above, this is closely tied to the prophet's ability to recognize the presence of God, the first textural component. The way that prophets respond to failure is a key factor that impacts future prophetic experiences. While participants speak of failures in the past, they logically follow the prophetic moment and thus will be treated last.

1. The Prophet's Mentoring:

"He Was a Tremendous Mentor to Me in the Spirit Realm" (P7)

The first structural factor that influences the experience of CP is mentoring. The phenomenon of CP never manifests without a prior teaching or mentoring relationship. The interviews indicate that mentoring comes from three different places: personal mentors, prophets within the local church, and popular prophetic leaders. It is worth noting that three of the participants had mentors from two of these categories. The most common type of mentorship was the personal mentor. "It's a relational thing," said P1, "Paul and Timothy, Moses and Joshua, Ruth and Naomi." P4 went on a prophetically-oriented trip to Israel, where she learned to prophesy from respected mentors whom she had a personal relationship with. P7 spoke of his uncle, a "very godly man." He was "a tremendous mentor to me in the spirit realm . . . Whenever I would go to his house, his Bible was open and he, as soon as I came to the door, he pushes everything back and him and I would talk about . . . the Lord and talk about Scripture and talk about giftings and dreams and visions God would show him." P8 learned from his own father, who experienced prophecy in a similar way:

> I watched my dad in life, the same thing would happen. He'd come home and tell us stories about, you know, he'd drive his truck . . . (he was the road superintendent). He wouldn't be able to turn one way, and he'd say, "God, what?" "Turn right." And he'd turn and there'd be a person on the side of the road there in tears and he would go and minister to them and it's incredible.

This participant's regular experience of prophetic inspiration was a more natural day-to-day occurrence rather than something tied to a prayer and worship setting. His method of prophecy echoes that of his mentor, something evident with all participants. Second, two of the participants learned to prophecy by witnessing the gift in action by people in their own congregation. P4 said, "The signal [that the prophetic inspiration was present] before I knew any appropriate terms for it, accurate terms, the signal was when Grandma Peterson [began to speak in tongues]. She was my signal." P7 also learned from prophets in his own congregation but in a different way. For a "season," God would tell him who was about to give a message in tongues and who would interpret. "I would just wait, and sure enough, Fred would give a message. Bill would interpret . . . [The Lord] did that a lot with me for probably a year." It was this preparation that gave the participant confidence to "step into" prophetic ministry when the Lord inspired him. Third, P1 quickly described a list of popular prophetic leaders who have influenced her through their books and YouTube videos: Graham Cooke, Rick Joyner, Kansas City Prophets, John Paul Jackson, Chris Vallotton, and James Goll. This list was by no means exhaustive. She ended the list by saying, "Uh, there are so many of them!" This participant had a clear appetite for prophetic things and found various American modern prophetic streams to satisfy her hunger.

2. The Prophet's Location

"Okay, What's Going on Here . . . Is the Good Stuff, Right?" (P6)[30]

The prophetic moment does not usually arrive ex nihilo. Participants regularly describe a setting—an "atmosphere" (P1, P7) that is conducive to prophecy. This setting is often pre-service prayer, the song service, the altar service, or a prayer meeting.[31] "I would find myself in church some Sunday mornings, like, . . . you get the atmosphere that you know there's going to be a message in tongues or there's an interpretation coming" (P7). P1 noted that prophetic inspiration occurred frequently during a time of spiritual renewal where there was a "high level of faith." This high level of faith led the congregation to expect that God would make his presence known prophetically. P6 describes walking into a worship service in a new town for the first time and realizing that "it's like walking into a room, and it's like, this is a place of encounter, like encountering the presence of the Lord Jesus through the power of the Holy Spirit." P2 remarked that this atmosphere was more readily found in aboriginal communities than in large urban centers because aboriginal communities "were very heightened in the spirit realm." This type of atmosphere is marked by a common purpose—"one frame of mind" (P7)—where the majority of the participants are open to the prophetic word, along with any other spiritual gift. Reflecting on the ease at which a faith-filled united atmosphere facilitates prophecy, P7 said that although God can use him prophetically in any situation, the right atmosphere makes prophesying easier. "I find in those settings the Lord really deals with me and, ah, I guess something in my spirit is more open at the time." It was during this sort of atmosphere that participants recognized the presence of God.

The role of time, unscripted moments, and waiting is a significant part of the prophetic location. Prophecy often occurs during an unscripted space in the worship service. This time is regularly found between the end of the planned praise and worship songs and the beginning of the sermon.

30. This comment described the participant's reaction when entering a charismatic-style praise and worship event where he understood that gifts of the Spirit would likely be welcomed.

31. By "altar service," I refer to the time common in Classical Pentecostal churches where people are invited to come to the following the sermon when people are invited to come to the front of the church to pray and respond to the message. See Samuel, *Holy Spirit*, 173–80.

P2 describes this moment vividly: "So a worship leader, she was leading . . . beautifully. And . . . God was, like, *not done*. You know, in a service that's not done? You sing the same song, but not repetitively boring. But you're actively engaging." P3 picks up on this same experience: "There comes a moment where there's a waiting period where people . . . almost anticipate that someone will have a word. So it's . . . weird because it's an unspoken liturgy that happens in Pentecostal circles, but everyone knows it." P3, a preacher, allows space inside his sermon outline to facilitate the prophetic impulse: "I always have gaps in my sermons . . . My gaps in the sermons are always for the Holy Spirit to fill the gaps. So often I'll end up telling a story or say a tidbit that I didn't plan. And it was . . . always for somebody." Prophets have an acute sense of timing and value the significance of waiting.

The atmosphere of faith and expectancy described in the previous paragraph is the regular context in which CP is experienced by the participants. However, it is not the *only* context. God's unexpected arrival in daily life was another underlying theme in the interviews. Participants speak about receiving the prophetic impulse while praying for people in Walmart (P5), or in a tractor or tree stand (P8). P8 feels more comfortable prophesying outside of the church setting because in church there is the temptation to be noticed. Some participants noted that the emotional state of the prophet is no barrier to prophetic inspiration. P3 spent the first half of the interview explaining prophetic moments that occurred during conductive atmospheres. However, when I asked him if God ever inspired him prophetically outside the church, he replied, "I experience Jesus on the street and arenas outside the church *far more* . . . Some of the Spirit-led moments are these, . . . just mundane things. Walking through the street, turn a corner [and] someone's there for me to pray with." For other participants, a worship service atmosphere makes it easier to prophesy because "you don't have any walls [up]. You say, 'I just want to receive' and then God just . . . pours it in because you're so flexible" (P5). It is clear from the interviews that there is no prerequisite atmosphere for prophecy. While a number of participants find it easier to prophecy in a faith-filled setting, a posture of attentiveness to God, described in the first textural section above, enables the prophet to recognize the presence of God and receive the prophetic impulse in any location.

3. *The Prophet's Response to Failure*

"You're Gonna Make Mistakes and Fail —That's Just a Given" (P1)

The final contextual component of CP that influences the way practitioners experience the phenomenon is their view of failure. Six of the eight participants chose to reflect on times when they have failed prophetically and how that has led them to experience the phenomenon in richer ways.[32] P1 and P8 clearly state the inevitability of failure when practicing CP. P8 reflected on a time when his pastor made a decision to let people practice spiritual gifts *knowing* the cost of that decision: "That would cause him a lot of pain, . . . there's lots of people make mistakes . . . But he allowed a lot of men and women to come alive spiritually that a lot of pastors would not find [themselves] comfortable doing." When participants reflect on mistakes in prophetic ministry, they do so in the context of looking forward to what those mistakes taught them. In this way, mistakes are viewed in a positive light. That is not to say that mistakes are not painful at the time. P5 explains how "God raised me all throughout these years and there were times when I was just like, I'm not even doing this again." This emotion was prompted by some prophetic messages the participant delivered that were not received well. However, she took the long perspective, using the language of "lifetime" twice. Mistakes, despite the pain, are opportunities to grow. It was a moment of failing to share a prophecy that gave P3 the courage to always share the message, regardless of the personal cost. He relates a time when he sensed the voice of God speaking to him and wrote the message down, engaging in personal discernment to determine whether he should share it or not. While this was happening, another person prophesied something that missed "the tone of the room." Following the service P3 spoke to the pastor who confirmed that the message he had written down was the true prophetic word for the church that morning. This missed opportunity was his "last lesson, . . . 'Okay, no matter what the situation is, what the circumstances are, if prompted, go do it." P4 and P8 state it clearly: "I missed quite a few [prophetic messages]. I have no idea how many I missed" (P4) and "God, did I miss an opportunity" (P8)? Again, these moments of candid self-reflection motivate these participants to be more attentive in the future. P4 recollects crying out in prayer, "'Oh,

32. Participants were not led in this direction by the interviewer. Failure was not in any of the potential prompts listed in the "Additional Interview Questions" (appendix 1).

I'm so sorry! You have to go on to somebody else,' and then the Lord would say, 'No actually, this is one of the best ways I can train you.'"

Structural Description Summary

The three structural components that influence the prophetic experience have been described in the words of the participants. While these components are not fundamental to the essence of the phenomenon, they directly impact the experience and will be woven together with the textural components in the following section to create a composite synthesis of CP. The following chart summarizes the structural components.

Structural Component	Features of the Component
1. Mentoring	A) Personal mentors B) Other prophets from the congregation C) Popular prophetic leaders
2. Setting	A) Prayer and worship context B) Timing and space C) Prophecy in the world
3. Failure	A) Inevitability B) Opportunities for growth

A Note on Time

Charts have been used at the end of the textural and structural section of this chapter to summarize and clarify what was discussed above. The use of these charts can have the inadvertent effect of making the components of CP appear to be neatly temporally ordered. This is not the case. Describing the experience of time has been a core component of phenomenology since Husserl.[33] Not just the world itself, but the way that humans *experience* the

---

33. See, e.g., Husserl, *On the Phenomenology of the Consciousness of Internal Time.*

world is temporally structured.[34] In each moment, humans retain previous moments and anticipate future moments.[35] All eight participants in this study described their experience with CP in ways that reveal how they experienced the temporality of the phenomenon. Dedicated reflection on the temporal relationships of the textural and structural components will illuminate how the phenomenon is perceived in time.

First, consider the structural components. The three structural elements of mentoring, setting, and failure, may be considered as a temporal backdrop that extends before and continues after the phenomenon proper. The prophets' past mentoring influences the way that they prophesy that in turn provides experience for future mentoring. The setting of the phenomenon, whether conducive or hindering, contribute to the experience of CP, enabling the prophet to become more aware of how the setting impacts their gift in the future. Failure is experienced as learning opportunities in the prophet's past but also as future potentialities that will in turn provide more opportunities for reflection. Like the drone note on a bagpipe that anchors the key of the melody, these three structural components are a temporal constant, anchoring and informing successive moments of prophetic inspiration.

The five textural components have only one clearly defined temporal relationship. That is, the prophet must *receive* the prophetic inspiration prior to *releasing* the prophetic message.[36] This temporal relationship can be near-simultaneous, such as when participants begin to speak under prophetic inspiration without knowing the full message. There can also be a significant delay between *reception* of the message and *release*. This is illustrated by the time when a participant *received* a message from the Lord that was *released* in a worship service months later. Regardless of the amount of time, *receiving* prophetic inspiration always logically precedes *releasing* the message. The prophet's *recognition* of the presence of God can occur at any time during CP, but it always occurs during the *receiving* of prophetic inspiration. Sometimes, especially in spiritually conducive settings, the prophet *recognizes* the presence of God prior to *receiving* the prophetic impulse. Other

---

34. Gallagher, *Phenomenology*, 102.

35. Husserl's model of time-consciousness describes the present moment as the "primal impression" that looks to the past through "retention" and toward the future through "protention." See Gallagher, *Phenomenology*, 103–107, for a clear description of Husserl's model.

36. In this section, the five key verbs from the textural components chart above have been italicized to clarify which component is being discussed.

times, the prophet may be caught off guard when the *recognition* of the presence of God and the *reception* of the prophetic impulse occur simultaneously. This is often the case in non-conducive settings. The *recognition* of the presence of God is unpredictable. It is regularly experienced throughout the entire prophetic experience. Some participants *recognized* the presence of God even when retelling stories of past prophetic events during the interview process. The *experience* of emotional or physical sensations occur at any time throughout the prophetic event. These sensations may occur simultaneously with the *recognition* of the presence of God and reoccur even when the experience is recalled years after the initial event. In addition to the ubiquity of the prophet's experience of physical and emotional sensations, it should be noted that these experiences intensify during the *releasing* of the prophetic message. Finally, there is the textural component of *discernment*. The discernment process may begin as soon as the prophet *recognizes* the presence of God and continue through the *reception, releasing,* and emotional *experiences* that accompany the prophetic event. A broader temporal progression was noted in discernment. As the participants practiced prophesying, the need for a formal conscious discernment process diminished as a more intuitive understanding took its place.

Synthesis of Textural and Structural Descriptions

The final step in phenomenological research is "the intuitive integration of the fundamental textural and structural descriptions into a unified statement of the essences of the experience of the phenomenon as a whole."[37] This composite description will be written in the form of a first-person narrative, a method outlined by Les Todres and demonstrated by Marcia Stanley Wertz et al.[38] Todres designed this method as a way to bridge the "complementary tension between academic and more narrative/poetic forms of writing," the second of which resonate more closely with human existence.[39] Wertz et al. summarize the method well:

> The composite first person narrative is a reflective story. It draws a composite picture of the phenomenon emerging from the informants. The composite is not a simple re-telling. It is interpretation

37. Moustakas, *Phenomenological Research Methods*, 100.

38. See Todres, *Embodied Enquiry*, and Wertz et al., "Composite First Person Narrative."

39. Todres, *Embodied Enquiry*, 45.

by the researcher in several important ways: through her knowledge of the literature regarding the phenomenon under enquiry,
through listening and hearing the stories told by the informants,
and through her own reflexivity during the process.[40]

The following composite description is not exhaustive. Indeed, given the
rich interplay between the essential textural components of the phenomenon and the structural variables, no one narrative will exhaust the experience.[41] However, this imaginative version of a prophetic experience does
aim to faithfully retell the phenomenon, drawing deeply on the experience and language of the participants while consciously bracketing the
researcher's preunderstandings. This final description will also serve as a
conclusion to this chapter, tying each of the above sections together into
one evocative narrative.

Composite First-Person Description

I awoke a few minutes before my alarm. As consciousness slowly material-
ized, I recognized that this was Sunday and began to anticipate the morning worship service at Renew Church. The church posts its worship song
list in advance, so I knew we were going to sing one of my favorites: "Holy
Spirit."[42] My small-group leader Ella and I share a love for this song. This
song helps her to open her heart to receive prophetic words from the Lord.
The song ran through my mind as I showered and prepared for church. By
the time I walked into the sanctuary, I could hardly wait for the worship
team to begin. I had this sense slowly building within my spirit that God
wanted to do something special this morning. From the first chord of the
first song, I locked in to worship. The noise of the people around me—the
crying child and the off-key singers—seemed to fade away as I felt the presence of the Holy Spirit surround me. And then they played *that* song. It's
like an informal liturgy in Renew Church: when you get to the slow songs,
you take time to pause, to linger. After singing through the verse and chorus
a few times, a simple I-IV chord progression on the synth pads filled the
room and the congregation began to pray extemporaneously. People began

40. Wertz et al., "Composite First Person Narrative," para. 7.

41. As Moustakas writes, "The essences of any experience are never totally exhausted"
(*Phenomenological Research Methods*, 100).

42. Torwalt and Torwalt, "Holy Spirit."

to sing in the Spirit—simple melodies that fit the chords.[43] Others began to pray in tongues, or just repeat the words "Jesus" or "Hallelujah." It was during this pause in the action, this unscripted moment of worship, that the Lord downloaded a short phrase into my spirit: "*Now* is the time." At first, I wondered how those words came into my mind—they have nothing to do with the song. The more I thought about them, the more I realized that this might be a message that God wants to share—wants *me* to share—with the church. The words would not go away. I felt my heart pounding as a strange pressure built in my chest, like I was in a river pushing against the current. Nervousness gave me pause. After all, four words is not much of a message! Then I remembered what happened during the worship service a few weeks ago. I had a similar sense that God had given me a message for the church, but I did not know what to do so I just waited. Eventually a person stood on the other side of the congregation and shared that *exact* message. It was not in the same words, but it meant the same thing. I was mortified at the time that I had let God down, but Ella encouraged me by saying that God was not angry—perhaps he's teaching me to be obedient. This time my respect for God and his word overcame my nerves so I stood to my feet and loudly declared, "*Now* is the time . . ." The message did not end after four words, though. It kept coming. As I continued to speak, the Spirit continued to place ideas in my mind to share with the congregation. This was real—God was here! In the end the message probably only took thirty seconds, but it felt like an hour. I was exhausted, like I had just returned from a long run! As I sat down to catch my breath, the pastor began to lead the congregation in a prayer of thanksgiving for the message. After the service, I was joking around with friends over coffee in the foyer when Ahmed came up to me. He told me that he was wrestling with a decision whether or not to leave his demanding job to free up time to be with his family and serve at the church. He told me that the words God spoke through me were *precisely* tuned to his situation and he now has the peace to know what to do next. I am so thankful that this time I took the opportunity and obeyed the voice of God.

43. To "sing in the Spirit" in Classical Pentecostalism means to sing in tongues. See Spittler, who notes that this understanding is rooted in Paul's injunction to "sing in the Spirit" (1 Cor 14:14–15) as a glossolalic act ("Glossolalia," 671). For a brief history of the phenomenon and a fascinating audio analysis, see Hinck, "Heavenly Harmony."

Chapter 5: Bringing Old and Contemporary Prophets Together

WITH THE RESULTS OF the literature review, the survey of Jeremiah's experience, and the original qualitative data from the phenomenological study in hand, we are able to attend to the crux of the practical theological work: theological reflection. To revisit Pattison and Woodward's definition from chapter 1, "Pastoral/practical theology is a place where religious belief, tradition and practice meets contemporary experiences, questions and actions and conducts a dialogue that is mutually enriching, intellectually critical, and practically transforming."[1] We have examined *religious belief, traditions*, and *practice* in the literature review (chapter 2) and the experience of Jeremiah (chapter 3). The phenomenological study (chapter 4) examined *contemporary prophetic experiences, questions* and *actions*, particularly in a Canadian PAOC/NL context. The remaining practical theological task is to conduct a *mutually enriching, intellectually critical, and practically transforming dialogue* between these two spheres. This will occur in the final two chapters of this book through the process of theological reflection. This chapter will explore areas of coherence between the Old Testament prophets and modern charismatic prophets. The final, concluding chapter will take that coherence one step further and suggest some areas where *mutually enriching dialogue* may occur.

In practical theology, theological reflection is fundamental to the overall work.[2] Edward Farley wrote about this in one of his pioneering essays in the field.[3] He makes the case that practical theology should be broadly defined as the interpretation of situations. One potential problem is that while we have methodological rigor in systematic theology,

---

1. Pattison and Woodward, "Introduction to Pastoral and Practical Theology," 7.

2. Osmer calls the work of this chapter the "normative task," when theological reflection is brought to bear on the situation under investigation (*Practical Theology*, 129–73).

3. Farley, "Interpreting Situations."

methodology for practical theology is less developed. Farley calls for an analysis of situations that is "self-conscious, self-critical, and disciplined."[4] That is, the same qualities expected in interpreting religious texts should be exhibited in the hermeneutical task of interpreting situations—in this case, the phenomenon of CP. This chapter will use the rigorous theological reflection to explicitly answer the research question: *How does the practice of CP in the PAOC and the PAONL cohere with the experience of the Old Testament prophets?* Six fruitful areas for investigation have been discovered where the coherence (or lack thereof) between Old Testament prophets and modern-day charismatic prophets come to a head. These are organized on a scale from the most significant challenges to coherence to the greatest support for coherence:

1. *Recognizing and Receiving*: Why do modern-day charismatic prophets recognize the presence of God before receiving the prophetic impulse when it happened simultaneously for Jeremiah?

2. *The Practice of Discernment*: Who is responsible for discerning the source and recipient of the message—the prophet or the recipients?

3. *The Authority of Scripture*: How highly do prophets value Scripture in relation to the prophetic word?

4. *The Invasive Inspiration*: Is the prophetic message something that the prophets formulate and craft or does it come from elsewhere?

5. *An Awkward Releasing*: Why do prophetic experiences often result in awkward circumstances?

6. *An Intense Sacramental Experience*: What role do physical and emotional sensations play in the prophetic experience?

This chapter will conclude by summarizing the significant amount of coherence between the Old Testament prophets and modern-day charismatic prophets.

1. Recognizing and Receiving

There is one clear area where the experience of the Old Testament prophets does not appear to cohere with the textural description of modern-day charismatic prophets. That point of tension is the distinction of *recognizing*

4. Farley, "Interpreting Situations," 10.

the presence of God prior to *receiving* the prophetic impulse. There is no evidence that Jeremiah recognized the presence of God in a way that was distinct from his reception of the prophetic word.[5] Jeremiah's prophetic message (and sign-act) to the Rechabites is a typical example of how Jeremiah received the prophetic impulse: "The word that came to Jeremiah from the LORD in the days of King Jehoiakim son of Josiah of Judah: Go to the house of the Rechabites, and speak to them . . ." (Jer 35:1–2). There was no recorded initial feeling or recognition of the presence of God prior to the reception of the prophetic impulse. The divine word came to Jeremiah and that was that! By way of contrast, consider how P7 described the significance of recognizing the presence of God *before* receiving the prophetic impulse: "I would find myself in church some Sunday mornings, like, you know, you get the atmosphere that you know there's going to be a message in tongues or there's an interpretation coming." For P7, being present in a context of worship and prayer was a preliminary step to his prophetic experience. Although some participants were surprised by the prophetic impulse (like Jeremiah) outside of a favorable context, the norm was to be in an "atmosphere" where the potential for receiving the prophetic word increased. How can we account for this lack of coherence between the experience of the Old Testament prophets and modern-day charismatic prophets? Four potential answers arise from the research: Jeremiah's unique role as an inspired writer of Scripture, the experience of time, a linguistic consideration, and structural differences. Each potential answer will be evaluated before a conclusion is drawn.

First, there is no question that Jeremiah was a unique prophet. He was called by God to become a prophet to the nations before he was conceived (Jer 1:5). The shattering power of the divine word of God was so significant

---

5. There is one possible exception to this. Jeremiah 23:18 reads: "For who has stood in the council of the Lord / so as to see and hear his word? / Who has given heed to his word so as to proclaim it?" Wessels writes: "True prophets receive a commission from Yahweh . . . They receive the message by coming into his council, where they receive the message by hearing, seeing and grasping Yahweh's word to his people" (Wessels, "Prophet versus Prophet," 744). The idea of standing in the divine council to hear a word from the Lord may suggest that Jeremiah experienced the council before receiving the prophetic impulse. The sensing of Yahweh's presence for Wessels has to do with "perception, awareness and feeling" (Wessels, "Prophetic Sensing," 5). However, Wessels goes on to say, reflecting Ellen G. White (*Yahweh's Council*), that "the presence of humans in the divine council is exceptional and allows access to prophets only rarely" ("Prophetic Sensing," 8). Therefore, while evocative, it is unwise to build a case based on this event that is rare even among the prophets.

in his life that word-language pushed spirit-language out of the book.[6] This unique calling and experience of the divine word empowered Jeremiah and his scribe Baruch to write down words that would become canonical Scripture. No modern-day charismatic prophet can claim such a pedigree! That Jeremiah wrote inspired and authoritative Scripture is the point on which Grudem argues for a clear distinction between Old Testament prophets and modern-day charismatic prophets. For Grudem, Old Testament prophets (and New Testament apostles) speak "God's very words," while modern-day charismatic prophets speak "something God brings to mind."[7] Therefore, there is a qualitative difference between the experience of Jeremiah and modern-day prophets. While there is no question that Jeremiah was a unique prophet (whether or not Grudem's logic is followed), the question remains whether that uniqueness is the reason why Jeremiah did not record recognizing the presence of God before receiving the prophetic word. Furthermore, does that uniqueness disqualify modern-day charismatic prophets from experiencing the divine word in a way congruous with Jeremiah?[8] In the qualitative research, some participants recorded receiving the prophetic impulse simultaneously with recognizing the presence of God. This leads us to the second potential answer.

Logically speaking, every time Jeremiah received the prophetic impulse, he *simultaneously* recognized the presence of God. That is, God was not absent from his word. The overwhelming quality of the divine word left Jeremiah no doubt that it was God's word he was stewarding. In the qualitative research, it was P8 who regularly received the prophetic impulse unexpectedly. Like Jeremiah, P8 regularly experienced the first two textural elements of CP simultaneously. His description of the prophetic experience makes this clear: "I could be driving along on my way to work and, . . . sometimes I feel this overwhelming presence. I don't hear a loud, audible voice . . . but I feel the Lord tell me, 'you need to this.' And [I have] this overwhelming sense that I have to do it."[9] These two elements:

6. Shead, *Mouth Full of Fire*, 266–69.

7. Grudem, *Gift of Prophecy*, 21, 27, 95. See the more complete discussion of Grudem's view above in chapter 2.

8. To be clear, this is not to suggest that modern-day charismatic prophets could receive messages with the authority of canonical Scripture. As seen in the literature review (chapter 2), the majority view of the theoretical literature is clearly against this, as is the confessional position of the PAOC (PAOC, "Contemporary Prophets," 5).

9. In the context of the interview, P8 was speaking about driving down a different road than usual that led him to encounter people to whom God inspired him to speak.

the "overwhelming presence" and "overwhelming sense" that he had to act bring the first two textural components of prophecy into temporal unison. The experience of P8 was a minority voice in the research, but in phenomenological research, significance does not depend on frequency. P8's experience provides a potential way beyond the apparent lack of coherence between the Old Testament prophets and modern-day charismatic prophets. One more element of P8's experience is significant—his bias against "fleshly" prophecy occurring in corporate worship gatherings: "I shy away from [prophesying in corporate worship gatherings]. In church services, I think (well, I shouldn't say this), . . . there are people that really want to be noticed, and they really want to be heard."[10]

A third explanation involves a linguistic consideration. Although not explicitly recorded, there is potential that the formulaic phrase "The Word of the Lord that came to . . ." (Hos 1:1, Joel 1:1; Mic 1:1) refers to a broader prophetic experience that might include recognizing the presence of God. In the context of another Old Testament prophet, Hosea, Hans Walter Wolff explains that this phrase does not refer directly to the revelatory words that follow but apply to the entire prophetic experience recorded in the book.[11] That would mean that the various subgenres that make up the book—divine commands, prophetic narratives, etc.—are all subsumed under this category.[12] Specific to Jeremiah, Holladay notes that the expression "the word of the Lord came" (Jer 1:4) also refers to more than just the specific content of the proceeding message.[13] Since the phrase is repeated in vv. 11 and 13, context shows that this expression covers both verbal prophecy and visionary material. Holladay writes about the expansive nature of this expression: "The phrase carries with it the whole paradoxical experience of the overwhelming inbreaking of God's revelation into the consciousness of the one who is to speak and act for God."[14] It is certainly possible although ultimately unprovable to suggest that Jeremiah did recognize the presence

---

10. P8 understands "fleshly prophecy" as prophecy that is prompted not from God but from the prophet's own mind. This understanding is analogous to the way prophets in Jeremiah who spoke "visions of their own mind" (Jer 23:16).

11. Wolff, *Hosea*, 4.

12. Wolff, *Hosea*, 4.

13. Holladay, *Jeremiah 1*, 32.

14. Holladay, *Jeremiah 1*, 32.

of God prior to receiving the prophetic impulse and that this process is subsumed under the stock prophetic formula.[15]

A fourth and final potential answer to the apparent lack of coherence between the experience of the Old Testament prophets and modern-day charismatic prophets considers the impact of structural differences. In the phenomenological study above, five structural and three textural elements of prophecy were discerned. The three structural elements (context, mentoring, and response to failure) refer to those elements that condition the way the phenomenon is experienced. Although they are described separately, texture and structure can never be separated. Ernest Keen writes: "It is not possible to describe texture without implicit notions of structure."[16] The structural elements provide the framework in which the textural elements of the phenomenon are experienced. When bringing the Old Testament prophets and modern-day charismatic prophets together in dialogue, the structural elements could not be more different. The experience of the research participants was influenced by the structural component of the setting in which the prophecy occurred. For most of the participants, that setting was a corporate worship gathering that included prayer and worship. This setting could be the reason why modern-day charismatic prophets tend to recognize the presence of God prior to receiving the prophetic impulse. It is commonplace for Pentecostal worshipers to recognize the presence of God in a corporate worship gathering. Jeremiah had no such favorable worship conditions! On the contrary, he prophesied during the dying days of a monarchy destined to be overrun by foreign powers. Temple worship was corrupted by the idolatrous political vacillations of the kings. There was no pleasant "atmosphere" for Jeremiah to become aware of the presence of God. This fundamental structural difference could be a major reason why Jeremiah did not recognize the presence of God before receiving the divine impulse. Interestingly, the one research participant (P8) who experienced prophecy in a manner more consistent with Jeremiah's experience was biased against corporate worship gatherings. With the structural element of setting more aligned between Jeremiah and P8, their experience of the textural components similarly aligned.

15. In a practical theological context, this observation would be part of the mutually beneficial dialogue between the Old Testament prophets and modern-day charismatic prophets. This implication will be considered further in the final chapter.

16. This quotation is from Moustakas, who cites an unpublished manuscript written in 1975 by Keen, entitled *Doing Research Phenomenologically* (Moustakas, *Phenomenological Research Methods*, 79).

Upon more thorough reflection, the experience of recognizing the presence of God and receiving the prophetic impulse may indeed cohere on this point. The experience of P8 has demonstrated that it is the structural differences between Jeremiah's day and modern-day that contribute to a different textural experience of prophecy. While Jeremiah certainly was unique as an author of Scripture, that uniqueness does not preclude modern-day charismatic prophets from experiencing prophecy in a similar manner.

2. The Practice of Discernment

Discernment is an area where there is only questionable coherence between the experience of the Old Testament prophets and modern-day charismatic prophets. For today's prophets, questions of discernment were front of mind in the phenomenological interviews—all eight participants were eager to describe their discernment process without leading questions. Participants explained two different types of discernment: discerning whether the prophetic impulse was from God and determining who the recipients of the prophetic message should be. These two discernment practices were engaged in both individually and with others, depending on the context.

By way of contrast, Jeremiah never engages in a process to discern whether the divine word he received is from God. The divine word was so powerful and consuming, it appears to be self-authenticating. That is, it is nowhere recorded that Jeremiah questions the source of the message. Jeremiah also had no need to discern who the recipient of the prophetic message should be since that direction was regularly included in the reception of the prophetic impulse. A typical example of this can be found in God's message to King Zedekiah during Nebuchadrezzar's attack: "Thus says the LORD, the God of Israel: Go and speak to King Zedekiah of Judah and say to him: Thus says the LORD . . ." (Jer 34:1–2). In this passage, both discernment questions are answered without any recorded discernment process: Yahweh is the source and King Zedekiah is the intended recipient.[17]

While the lack of a discernment process in Jeremiah's experience is a clear divergence from the experience of modern-day charismatic prophets, the issue of discernment is raised in the book of Jeremiah in the confrontation between Jeremiah and Hananiah (Jer 27–28). While not

17. As mentioned above, it is possible that Jeremiah engaged in a personal or corporate discernment process that has not been recorded. Unfortunately, because there is no way to return to the pre-textual experience, speculation would be futile.

an explicit discernment process, Jeremiah does appeal to the prophetic tradition to support his message:

> Listen now to this word that I speak in your hearing and in the hearing of all the people. The prophets who preceded you and me from ancient times prophesied war, famine, and pestilence against many countries and great kingdoms. As for the prophet who prophesies peace, when the word of that prophet comes true, then it will be known that the LORD has truly sent that prophet. (Jer 28:7–9)

Jeremiah argues that since prophets regularly prophesy negative words, the burden of proof lies with the prophet who prophesies peace. In this situation, the burden of discernment is placed squarely on the audience who received the conflicting prophetic messages and sign-acts. The audience were the ones tasked with how to respond to two biblical messages with no time to wait to see which prophetic message would be historically validated. Since the phenomenological study focused exclusively on the experience of *prophets*, not their *audience*, it is impossible to determine the extent to which recipients of modern-day CP assume the role of discernment. A future study that correlated both the prophetic message and its reception by the audience would be required to make that determination.

Although Jeremiah does not explicitly discern the source or recipients of his own prophetic message, we do see him boldly calling out the false prophets around him. Consider God's message through Jeremiah to the exiles in Babylon who believed they may soon return to Jerusalem: "For thus says the LORD of hosts, the God of Israel: Do not let the prophets and the diviners who are among you deceive you, and do not listen to the dreams that they dream, for it is a lie that they are prophesying to you in my name; I did not send them, says the LORD" (Jer 29:8–9). While Jeremiah appears certain of his own ability to hear God's true voice, he is quick to call out the false messages of other prophets. In this way, he practices discernment—albeit the discernment of others.

There was one hint in the phenomenological study that provides a modest case for coherence on this point. P7 spoke about maturing in prophetic ministry. He highly valued a pastor in his life who allowed him (and others) to develop their spiritual gifts. The Lord told his pastor "that in his stall . . . there were a lot of stallions. And he could open up the gate and let them run [and] let them learn and let them grow under his ministry in the supernatural giftings." As P7 grew in his prophetic gift, the explicit discernment process he relied on in his early life was not as necessary. Instead, "when you have a relationship with someone, you recognize their voice over other voices" (P7). Perhaps Jeremiah's relationship with God was so highly developed, no explicit discernment process was needed. One might speculate that Jeremiah's ability to discern God's voice clearly was a gift related to his role as an author of Scripture. Of course, the option remains that the moments of personal discernment are simply not recorded in the final text. On this point we can go no further. To sum up the question of discernment, it is an area of contrast between Jeremiah and modern-day charismatic prophets, although there are potential ways forward, including further exploration of the requirement of modern-day recipients to discern and the question of increasing maturity leading to a decrease in the need for an explicit discernment process.

3. The Authority of Scripture

Jeremiah's prophecies were spoken, written, redacted, and have come to be viewed as authoritative Scripture in both the Jewish and Christian traditions. In this, Jeremiah is different from modern-day charismatic prophets. However, there is a deeper level of coherence to be explored. Jeremiah and modern-day charismatic prophets both highly value God's word in their prophetic ministries. Upon first glance, this point may seem too obvious to raise—prophets are people who speak God's voice, not their own! That said, the literature review has demonstrated a significant amount of concern about the level of authority that prophetic messages carry.[18] A closer look at this area of coherence will address this concern. Jeremiah, like modern-day charismatic prophets, is deeply rooted in Scripture.

Scholars have noted Jeremiah's coherence with the Deuteronomic tradition.[19] Allen notes that the prose sermons of Jeremiah are "often but

18. Recall how Grudem describes New Testament apostles as the true heirs to the Old Testament prophets based on the criteria of who can write authoritative Scripture (Grudem, *Gift of Prophecy*, 27–49). It is also significant that Pentecostal scholar Robeck in the widely recognized *New International Dictionary of Pentecostal and Charismatic Movements* concludes his article on the gift of prophecy with discussion on the limits of prophetic authority: "Within the Christian tradition it must be limited by the teachings of Scripture as understood by the members of the community of faith as they seek to submit themselves one to another and to live under the guidance of Scripture as the ultimate written authority in all matters of faith and practice" ("Prophecy," 1012).

19. It should be noted here that there are significant diachronic questions that could

by no means always" taken from Deuteronomy.[20] Jeremiah's sermon in the temple court (7:1—8:3) is one example that demonstrates the influence of Deuteronomy in Jeremiah's prophetic ministry. In vv. 21–29, Jeremiah argues that God never commanded burnt offerings and sacrifices when God's people were brought out of Egypt. Rather, they were commanded thus: "Obey my voice, and I will be your God, and you shall be my people; and walk only in the way that I command you, so that it may be well with you" (7:23). This point echoes Deut 10:12: "So now, O Israel, what does the LORD your God require of you? Only to fear the LORD your God, to walk in all his ways, to love him, to serve the LORD your God with all your heart and with all your soul." Here, the command to "walk" in obedience is recontextualized by Jeremiah.[21]

Jeremiah's rootedness in the Deuteronomic tradition is also underscored by the metaphor of eating:

> Your words were found, and I ate them,
>> And your words became to me a joy
>> And the delight of my heart;
> For I am called by your name,
>> O LORD, God of hosts. (Jer 15:16)

Interpreters differ on the referent to which "words" points. Miller argues that the words Jeremiah ate were "surely" the prophetic message placed in Jeremiah's mouth at his call.[22] However, the fact that the words "were found" evoke Hilkiah's discovery of the book of the law during the

---

be explored regarding the relationship between Jeremiah and Deuteronomy. Holladay refers to the relationship between Jeremiah and Deuteronomy as "one of the most persistent and intractable historical-critical questions in OT study" ("Elusive Deuteronomists," 55). Blenkinsopp speaks of the Deuteronomistic editing of the book of Jeremiah in which the editors portray Jeremiah as a true prophet raised up by God, with the words of God in his mouth (Deut 18:18; Jer 1:7, 9, 17) (*History of Prophecy in Israel*, 137). Potential historical reconstructions, while intriguing, are outside the scope of the canonical-literary approach adopted here. The final canonical form of the text portrays Jeremiah as a prophet who is rooted in Deuteronomic theology.

20. Allen, "Jeremiah, Book of," 426. Allen lists the locations of the prose sermons: 7:1—8:3; 11:1–14; 14:11–16; 18:7–12; 21:5–9; 22:1–5; 25:3–12; 26:3–6; 30:3, 8–9; 32:29–41; 34:8–22; 40:2–3; 44:2–10, 20–23 ("Jeremiah, Book of," 426).

21. Miller notes that "the influence of Deuteronomy may be felt at this point, for that same question about the Lord's requirements is answered there with words about fearing and serving the Lord and walking in the Lord's ways (Deut 10:12), just the point Jeremiah's prophecy makes" (*Jeremiah*, 639).

22. Miller, *Jeremiah*, 697.

renovation of the temple (2 Kgs 22:3–13). For this reason, Lundbom argues that Jeremiah ate the recently rediscovered words of the Torah.[23] This second interpretation strongly emphasizes the formative role of the Deuteronomic tradition in Jeremiah's prophetic ministry.[24]

The participants in the phenomenological study similarly emphasized the need to be thoroughly rooted in Scripture in a variety of ways. P4 reflected on the way that her biblical foundation supported her current prophetic ministry. "It is often said to me that . . . I trust you prophetically because you are so word-based and I have said back to that person, 'I trust me too!' And I am word-based. I am so thankful for those Sunday School teachers. I am so thankful." For her, like Jeremiah, years of "eating" Scripture have shaped her prophetic ministry. P8 found that God often used his regular Bible reading practice to fuel his prophetic ministry. "Often times I've said, 'God, give me a word,' and I've said, 'lead me,' and I've read . . . and the Lord has given me an exact word for an exact time for a person." Like P8, many of the participants have found that God brings Scripture to mind in their prophetic ministry. P2, for example, describes her reception of the prophetic impulse by stating how "a Scripture would come into my spirit."

The PAOC wrote that prophecy should be exercised "frequently and authentically within the protective boundaries of biblical accountability."[25] The way that Jeremiah and modern-day charismatic prophets are deeply rooted in and reliant upon authoritative scriptural tradition enables them to prophecy within scriptural boundaries. The that modern-day prophets may view their words as having a level of authority on par with Scripture is undermined by their continual reference to and dependency upon Scripture.

4. The Invasive Inspiration

Muindi used the term "invasive" in his description of CP.[26] This term vividly captures the nature of prophecy as a message that finds its source

---

23. Lundbom, "Jeremiah," 686.

24. In addition to the Deuteronomic tradition, we have explored above regarding the issue of discernment how Jeremiah also referenced the earlier prophetic tradition to support his words (Jer 28:7–9). It is unclear the extent to which any of the prophetic tradition during this time period were understood as canonical.

25. PAOC, "Contemporary Prophets," 7.

26. Muindi, "Nature and Significance," 255; Muindi, *Pentecostal-Charismatic Prophecy*, 224.

outside the one who speaks or acts. In short, prophets speak God's words, not their own. This is a clear area of coherence between Jeremiah and modern-day charismatic prophets. In a moment of dialogue between Jeremiah and God, the prophet complains that other prophets are delivering a message of peace—the opposite of Jeremiah's message. God informed Jeremiah that "the prophets are prophesying lies in my name; I did not send them, nor did I command them or speak to them. They are prophesying to you a lying vision, worthless divination, and *the deceit of their own minds*" (Jer 14:14, emphasis added). Rather than prophesy out of his own mind or imagination, Jeremiah consistently receives and delivers the invasive word of God. Shead makes the intriguing observation that "Jeremiah is never said to 'hear' God's words."[27] Rather, it is the word of God (singular) that comes to Jeremiah. While the same thing is communicated in both expressions, the biblical formulation puts Jeremiah in a passive position, receiving what comes from beyond him. It is not Jeremiah's ability to hear but God's ability to speak that matters.

Participants in the phenomenological study all similarly emphasized the invasive nature of the prophetic experience. P8 described the reception of the divine word thus: "I'll be honest, sometimes I'm not looking for it and I just feel the Lord speak." P3 said, "I felt the fire in my belly, and I sense a whisper in my ear of what needs to be said." P7 admits that when his mind wanders, "the Holy Spirit grabs a hold of [his] attention." In each of these three examples, the word of God is perceived as something that comes to the prophet from God—not something developed or cognitively prepared. P4 elaborates on this theme with a terse expression: "I like to say that prophecy begins in the ear. You should think of it as the mouth, you know? What am I going to say? What did that person just say? . . . Certainly, in my accumulated experience and even now [prophecy] begins in the ear." Her point was not that the prophet must strain to listen for the divine word. Rather, she was emphasizing the fact that prophecy does not come from *thinking* about what to say. Rather, the word arrives invasively, from God. In this way, the experience of Jeremiah and modern-day charismatic prophets cohere closely.

---

27. Shead, *Mouth Full of Fire*, 55. See also Lamb, who observes more generally: "Although one might expect that the prophetic mediator would experience the divine word primarily by hearing, this is not the primary method of communication that the text records. The prophet will command the eventual audience to hear the word of God, but in most prophetic books, often at the very beginning the divine word 'came' (*hāyâ*) to the prophet" ("Word of God," 861).

5. An Awkward Releasing

Both Jeremiah and modern-day charismatic prophets release the prophetic word in similar modes. Jeremiah used the medium of speech, the written word, and sign-acts to prophesy. The same is true with research participants. While everyone releases the prophetic messages vocally, many also write those messages down. P2 writes prophetically inspired songs, P5 journals when she wakes up to record any prophetically inspired dreams, and P4 writes prophetic messages down and distributes them widely by email. While sign-acts were rarer among research participants, P1 asked her husband to dance with her in church and P4 shared an incident regarding the pantomime of an invisible sword.[28] That these three modes of releasing the prophetic word cohere is not surprising—prophets by nature are required to communicate the prophetic impulse. What is more significant is the theme of awkwardness.

Jeremiah released the prophetic message in socially awkward ways that would have the potential to embarrass him. He wore an unwashed loincloth to show how God would "ruin the pride of Judah and the great pride of Jerusalem" (Jer 13:8). He refused to marry or demonstrate grief for those who died (Jer 16:1–9). In a socially uncouth moment, he offered wine to the Rechabites—a people who vowed to drink no wine (Jer 35:1–19). In addition to these sign-acts, the content of his messages was consistently countercultural, challenging the authority of the monarchy and the comfort of the common people. The Old Testament prophets were consistently out of step with polite society while remaining in step with the demands of God who spoke through them.

The same can be said of modern-day charismatic prophets. Participants regularly report awkward moments where they must choose whether to sacrifice comfort and politeness in order to faithfully release the prophetic message. P3 spoke about the awkwardness of bringing a stern prophetic message to a room full of leaders with more structural authority than him. P8 records a time when he was prophetically inspired to share a passage of Scripture with his senior pastor that could be interpreted negatively. The pastor broke into tears and said, "The three things the Lord's been speaking to me this week are all in that verse. I never even knew that verse existed." P7 records that "moving in the prophetic sometimes, it takes you out on a limb,

28. Perhaps the rarity of prophetic sign-acts among research participants could be explained by a lack of familiarity with the Old Testament prophets—something this book seeks to remedy. This is something that this book seeks to remedy.

and that's not very comfortable." In addition to these, there's the memorable account of P4 singing at the top of her lungs during prayer time after the service, "How much is that doggy in the window?" This sort of training in awkwardness conditions prophets to value God's word more than the recipients of their prophetic messages or their own comfort. When P7 was asked if risk-taking during prophetic ministry led him to worry about how he would be perceived, he replied quickly, "Well, I don't care about that anymore. Yeah, I just don't care. Obedience matters to me more. So I don't care if other people reject me as long as I know that God is leading me and I'm living in obedience. It would have irked me more if I was prompted and didn't do anything." The requirement to press through awkwardness and obey is a clear area of coherence between the Old Testament prophets and modern-day charismatic prophets.

6. An Intense Sacramental Experience

The strongest area of coherence between the Old Testament prophets and modern-day charismatic prophets is the intensity of the actual prophetic experience. We have already reviewed some of the key verses that convey the intensity of Jeremiah's experience. Jeremiah describes his heart being "crushed," his bones "shaking," becoming like a "drunkard" when he received the prophetic impulse (Jer 23:9). He experiences the prophetic calling of God as an enticement or a seduction in which he is "overpowered" by God (Jer 20:7). He famously described the prophetic word as a "fire" that he must release lest it burn him from the inside (Jer 20:9).

It is significant that while all of the participants report feeling emotional and physical sensations associated with the prophetic event, three participants describe the intensity of the prophetic event using Jeremiah's language. P1, P3, and P5 all describe the feeling of pressure when God has given a prophetic word that must be released. P3 and P5 even use the term "fire" to describe the sensation. P3 speaks of breaking down into tears and being thoroughly "overwhelmed, emotionally [and] physiologically" by the prophetic event. Some prophetic experiences were so emotionally significant that participants re-experienced associated physical sensations like goose bumps during the interview that took place months or sometimes years after the event being remembered.

The sacramental-experiential model developed by Muindi's practical theological research on CP in Kenya faithfully describes the experience conveyed by Jeremiah and modern-day charismatic prophets:

> It was observed . . . that charismatic prophecy was perceived as an intense moment of a participatory interface between the divine spirit (the Holy Spirit) and the human deep unconscious dimension (the human spirit) and that the divine spirit overwhelmed and infused the human conscious dimension (the mind) with revelatory impulses. Such an intense participation of the human spirit in the divine Spirit is deemed to be a sacramental experience.[29]

This sacramental participation in the divine was described by Muindi's research participants in terms very similar to the participants in this study, despite the cultural difference between Canada and Kenya. Muindi's participants felt "physical sensations," an "overwhelming compulsion to speak," "a sense of being physically overpowered," "a feeling of overwhelming excitement," or "overwhelming joy."[30] These physical and emotional sensations of modern-day charismatic prophets, whether in Kenya or Canada, cohere directly with the physical and emotional sensations of Jeremiah and the Old Testament prophets in general.

Conclusion

To conclude, it will be helpful to recapitulate the preceding six points within the fivefold textural structure of the phenomenological experience of modern-day charismatic prophets. The first element is *recognizing* the presence of God. Unlike modern-day charismatic prophets who tend to *recognize* the presence of God in a worship service before *receiving* the divine impulse, Jeremiah always experienced these two textural components simultaneously. This difference can be accounted for by the structural difference in settings—Jeremiah had no conductive worship service in which he would *recognize* the presence of God before *receiving* the prophetic impulse. The fact that some participants experienced these two elements simultaneously like Jeremiah also argues for coherence. The second element is *receiving* the prophetic impulse. There is significant coherence here in that both Jeremiah and modern-day charismatic prophets highly value the authority of

29. Muindi, *Pentecostal-Charismatic Prophecy*, 186.

30. Muindi, *Pentecostal-Charismatic Prophecy*, 191.

Scripture. Furthermore, both experience the invasive inspiration of God that comes from beyond their own imaginations. The third element is *discerning* the source and recipient of the prophetic word. This element is the strongest lack of coherence since Jeremiah never explicitly engages in a personal discernment process. This lack of coherence may be partially mitigated by the point raised by P8 that increasing maturity results in a decreasing need for an explicit discernment process. The fourth element is *releasing* the prophetic message. There is strong coherence here both in the ways in which the message is released and the awkwardness that regularly must be pushed through en route to full obedience. The final element is the *experience* of attendant physical and emotional sensations. This is another area of strong coherence between Jeremiah and modern-day charismatic prophets. Both experience a sacramental intensity that results in similar emotional and physical responses. It is clear from the theological reflection in this chapter that the experience of modern-day charismatic prophets coheres strongly with the experience of the Old Testament prophets in many ways. Where there are experiences unique to Jeremiah, they are mitigated by the structural differences inherent in the cultural and historical distance between modern practitioners and the ancient Near East. In the final chapter we will use the areas of coherence explored here to bring the Old Testament prophets and modern-day charismatic prophets into the "mutually enriching" dialogue that lies at the heart of practical theology.[31]

---

31. Pattison and Woodward, "Introduction to Pastoral and Practical Theology," 7.

Chapter 6: Conclusion, Limitations, and Areas for Future Research

IT TAKES A SIGNIFICANT amount of motivation to sustain a project of this length. My motivation came from two places. First was my own experience with the phenomenon of prophecy. I am an unusual Pentecostal in that my disposition tends more toward reserved expressions of worship. That said, my experience with prophecy (as recorded at the start of chapter 4) was personally undeniable. The contradiction between my typical experience of God and that intense prophetic moment remained on my mind as I continued in pastoral ministry. When abuses of this spiritual gift would lead me toward cynicism, this prophetic event sustained my belief in the value and role of prophecy in the church. This experience made me curious, which brings me to the second motivating factor underlying this project. In an attempt to understand more deeply what I had experienced, I picked up Abraham Heschel's *The Prophets*. Here was a biblical scholar who accurately described my experience in vivid phenomenological language:

> The call to be a prophet is more than an invitation. It is first of all a feeling of being enticed, of acquiesce or willing surrender. But this winsome feeling is only one aspect of the experience. The other aspect is a sense of being ravished or carried away by violence, of yielding to overpowering force against one's own will. The prophet feels both the attraction and the coercion of God, the appeal and the pressure, the charm and the stress. He is conscious of both voluntary identification and forced capitulation.[1]

Although Heschel's book came out six decades ago, his concept of God's pathos resonated deeply with me on an experiential level. By God's *pathos*, Heschel speaks of "a form of relation,"[2] the way that God makes his passionate self known to the prophets. God's *pathos* is "the unity of the

1. Heschel, *Prophets*, 145.
2. Heschel, *Prophets*, 298.

eternal and the temporal, of meaning and mystery, of the metaphysical and the historical. It is the real basis of the relationship between God and man [*sic*], of the correlation of Creator and creation, of the dialogue between the Holy One of Israel and His people."[3] For Heschel, prophets do more than communicate a message: they *feel* the heart of God and respond in kind. This is what I believed I experienced that day leading worship when God broke me emotionally in front of the congregation and this was what I hoped to explore more deeply in this practice-led study.[4]

The research surprised me. As mentioned in chapter 4, none of the participants experienced the *pathos* of God in this way. Although every participant experienced some degree of physical and emotional sensation, these were never connected to the disposition of God in the prophetic moment. What I had intended to prove turned out to become little more than a footnoted validation strategy.[5] Despite this discouragement, there are areas where this research uncovered generative areas for further reflection. It is to this task that we now turn our attention.

Summary and Conclusions

This project set out to answer the question: *How does the practice of CP in the PAOC and PAONL cohere with the experience of the Old Testament prophets?* The phenomenological study resulted in a five-point textural description of the experience of modern-day charismatic prophets in the PAOC and PAONL, qualified by three structural components. Prophets *recognize* the presence of God, *receive* the prophetic impulse, *discern* the source and recipient of the message, *release* the prophetic message or act, and *experience* attendant physical and emotional sensations. The way that prophets experience this phenomenon is impacted by their *mentoring, setting,* and *response to failure.* A survey of the Old Testament prophets centered on the prophetic experience of Jeremiah revealed that Jeremiah experienced the prophetic phenomenon in a very similar way. With two possible exceptions, the Old Testament prophets and modern-day charismatic prophets deeply

---

3. Heschel, *Prophets*, 298. Heschel's work frequently blurs the line between poetry and prose, overwhelmed as he is in response to the divine *pathos*.

4. These two motivations prompted my article, "Sunday Morning Prophets."

5. That is, the research clarified researcher bias through reflexivity (Creswell and Poth, *Qualitative Inquiry*, 261).

cohere on an experiential level.[6] With this coherence in mind we turn to the "mutually enriching" dialogue between the experience of the Old Testament prophets and modern-day Charismatic prophets.[7]

How Does This Coherence Inform Modern-Day Charismatic Prophets?

The theoretical portion of the literature review (chapter 2) revealed that biblical scholars, including Pentecostal scholars, tend to emphasize the discontinuity between the Old Testament prophets and the New Testament gift of prophecy (and, by extension, modern-day CP). By emphasizing discontinuity, scholars are able to strongly uphold both the uniqueness of Jesus and the unique authority of Scripture. The unfortunate consequence of that emphasis is the subsequent disconnect of the Old Testament prophets from our contemporary experience. This research project has demonstrated that there is significant coherence between these two worlds that, when emphasized, will benefit the church. In order to see how this coherence will benefit the church, we must first consider Pentecostal theology.

Pentecostal theology is narrative in shape. In his entry in the Systematic Pentecostal and Charismatic Theology series, Vondey claims that while Pentecostalism is centered on the Pentecost as the chief "theological symbol," its theology is best described as having a narrative shape.[8] Unlike other streams of Christianity such as the Roman Catholic and Reformed traditions, Pentecostal theology resists dogmatic summarization. To understand Pentecostal doctrine, we must listen to how Pentecostals articulate their "theological story."[9] That story is known as the full gospel, described by Aimee Semple McPherson as follows: "Jesus saves us according to John 3:16. He baptizes us with the Holy Spirit according to Acts 2:4. He heals our bodies according to James 5:14–15. And Jesus is coming again to receive

---

6. The two possible exceptions are, first, that Jeremiah did not explicitly experience the first two textural components sequentially, and second, that the role of discernment functioned differently. These were explored in detail in the previous chapter.

7. Pattison and Woodward, "Introduction to Pastoral and Practical Theology," 7.

8. Vondey, *Pentecostal Theology*, 2.

9. Vondey, *Pentecostal Theology*, 21. Vondey further argues that "a theological symbol cannot function without a corresponding theological narrative," and that narrative "expands and articulates symbol" (*Pentecostal Theology*, 289).

us unto Himself according to 1 Thessalonians 4:16–17."[10] This full gospel story, the "plot of Pentecost," is "appropriated" through the practice of altar call and response.[11] It is at the altar where people in the early days of Pentecostalism "experienced the immediacy of God."[12] It was at the altar where Pentecostals relived the plot of salvation, sanctification, healing, Spirit-baptism, and excitement over Jesus' imminent return.

While the gift of prophecy was a fundamental experience of Pentecostalism from the beginning, it does not have a seat at the four- or fivefold full gospel narrative table. I believe that a recognizing of the coherence between CP and the Old Testament prophets enables us to expand our narrative vision to include the prophetic tradition that preceded Christ, came to a head in Christ, and was then passed on *via* the outpouring of the Spirit at Pentecost. In this way, the narrative theology of Pentecostalism has the potential to be far broader than traditionally understood. While appropriating the narrative of Pentecostalism, either at the altar or elsewhere, the gift of prophecy can serve to remind Pentecostals that our story coheres with Israel's story. With this understanding, I envision Pentecostals reading the Classical Prophets in a new light—mining the riches of (approximately) one-third of the Old Testament for insight into their spiritual ancestors. Texts that are primarily used for their messianic predictions or social justice emphases can now be read on a more sympathetically experiential level.

How Does This Coherence Inform Our Understanding of the Old Testament Prophets?

This side of the mutual enriching dialogue is more difficult to explore because Pentecostals with their high view of Scripture shy away from the idea that their experience could inform Scripture. That said, Pentecostals have historically reread the Acts narrative from the position of their own experience. Bradley Truman Noel expands on this theme:

> For the Pentecostal, Scripture must primarily speak to the modern
> reader; simply focusing on what the text may have originally meant

10. As quoted in Dayton, *Theological Roots of Pentecostalism*, 21. There is a fifth movement in the narrative: Jesus sanctifies. Dayton argues that while the fivefold pattern is "historically prior," the fourfold pattern "expresses more clearly and cleanly the logic of Pentecostal theology" (*Theological Roots of Pentecostalism*, 21).

11. Vondey, *Pentecostal Theology*, 37.

12. Samuel, *Holy Spirit*, 47.

> is not enough. The Pentecostal insists on closing the gap between the two horizons . . . Pentecostals contribute most substantially to hermeneutics in the area of experience and verification. Whereas Classical Pentecostalism tended to distinguish poorly between the horizons of reader and author, contemporary scholars rely on their own experience to bridge that gap.[13]

With that in mind, is it not possible that our reading of Jeremiah and the Old Testament prophets could be informed by the experience of modern-day charismatic prophets who, like their ancestors a century ago, read Acts 2 with fresh eyes having experienced Spirit-baptism firsthand? In the previous chapter I suggested that the expression "The word of the LORD came . . ." was broad enough to include the full experience of the prophet not necessarily narrated in detail in the text. Would it be too much of a stretch to suggest that Jeremiah and his contemporaries also recognized the presence of God prior to receiving the prophetic impulse? Scripture is silent on this matter so we must not be dogmatic. However, from a practical theological perspective, the connection is intriguing.

Limitations and Areas for Future Research

In any research project there are limitations and areas for future research and this project is no exception. There are at least three main limitations that should be noted that point toward areas for future research. First, this study focused on how modern-day charismatic prophets experienced the phenomenon of prophecy. No attention was given to the audience that received those messages, except through the perception of the prophets. Chapter 5 revealed some unanswerable questions about the nature of discernment and the responsibility of recipients in the process of discernment. A study of how the audience receives prophetic messages would be a welcome companion to this study. Second, the scope of the study was a limitation. Given that there were extant studies on prophecy in England, Kenya, and Singapore, I sought to explore the phenomenon in my own context of Canada. Still, many regions of the world with unique Pentecostal and charismatic expression have yet to be studied. As data emerges from more locations, our picture of global CP will become increasingly clear. Third, this study included a relatively brief chapter on Jeremiah's experience with some reference to other Old Testament prophets. I believe this was the best approach within

---

13. Noel, *Pentecostal and Postmodern Hermeneutics*, 164–65.

the limitations of this study because we have more personal data about Jeremiah than any other Old Testament prophet. That said, the prophetic corpus is far larger than any one chapter can describe. A full-scale biblical study of the experience of the Old Testament prophets would be a valuable way to further verify the level of coherence.

In the end, this study was deeply satisfying. Despite not confirming my initial presuppositions about how modern-day prophets experience the pathos of God, this study has clearly demonstrated the experiential coherence between the Old Testament prophets and the charismatic prophets of today. This has opened new vistas of understanding for both the Old Testament prophets as well as the prophets of today. It is my prayer that this study will spark a renewed interest in the Old Testament prophets in our PAOC and PAONL churches. Like Jeremiah, may we devour these words of Scripture (Jer 15:16) so they may nourish the gift of prophecy that is the spiritual birthright of those of us who live on this side of Pentecost.

Appendix 1
Additional Interview Questions

1. What do you feel before, during, and after a prophetic experience?

   - What emotions do you experience?

   - What does the inspiration of God feel like?

2. Has your practice of prophecy changed over the years?

   - How did you learn to prophesy?

   - How has it changed?

   - Have you noticed an increase or decrease in the amount of prophecy?

3. Describe the setting where and when you practice prophecy.

   - Worship service?

   - What time in the service?

   - Is there music playing?

4. Which Scriptures inform your understanding of prophecy?

   - New Testament passages?

   - The Hebrew prophets themselves?

5. What themes typically arise when you prophesy?

   - Positive, negative, mixed?

   - *Glossolalia?*

6. How do people respond to your prophecies?

   - The congregation?

   - The pastor?

Bibliography

Ahn, John. "Exile." In *DOP*, 196–204.

Åkerlund, Truls. *A Phenomenology of Pentecostal Leadership.* Eugene, OR: Wipf & Stock, 2018.

Allen, Leslie C. *Jeremiah: A Commentary.* Louisville: Westminster John Knox, 2008.

———. "Jeremiah: Book of." In *DOP*, 423–41.

Alter, Robert. *The Hebrew Bible: A Translation with Commentary.* 3 vols. New York: Norton, 1996–2019.

Archer, Kenneth J. "Early Pentecostal Biblical Interpretation." *Journal of Pentecostal Theology* 9 (2001) 32–70.

———. *A Pentecostal Hermeneutic: Spirit, Scripture and Community.* Cleveland: CPT, 2005.

Aune, David E. *Prophecy in Early Christianity and the Ancient Mediterranean World.* Eugene, OR: Wipf & Stock, 1983.

Baker, Daniel J. "The Complete Theological Program of Acts 2:17–21 in Luke-Acts." *Pneuma* 42 (2020) 50–67.

Ballard, Paul. "The Use of Scripture." In *The Wiley Blackwell Companion to Practical Theology*, edited by Bonnie J. Miller-McLemore, 163–72. Malden: Wiley Blackwell, 2014.

Barkley, Stephen. "Charismatic Prophecy in the Pentecostal Assemblies of Canada: An Old Testament Perspective." DPT diss., McMaster Divinity College, Hamilton, Ontario, 2022.

———. "Sunday Morning Prophets." *Enrich: The Leadership Magazine of the Pentecostal Assemblies of Canada* (2017) 9–12.

———. "Toronto Blessing." In *Brill's Encyclopedia of Global Pentecostalism Online*, edited by Michael Wilkinson et al., n.p. 2019. http://dx.doi.org/10.1163/2589-3807_EGPO_COM_040615.

Bartholomew, Theodore T., et al. "A Choir or Cacophony? Sample Sizes and Quality of Conveying Participants' Voices in Phenomenological Research." *Methodological Innovations* (2021) 1–14. https://doi.org/10.1177/20597991211040063.

Barton, John. "Postexilic Hebrew Prophecy." In *ABD*, 5:489–95.

Beal, L. Wray. "Literary Approaches." In *DOP*, 506–13.

Blenkinsopp, Joseph. *A History of Prophecy in Israel.* Rev. ed. Louisville: Westminster John Knox, 1996.

Boda, Mark J., and J. Gordon McConville, eds. *Dictionary of the Old Testament Prophets.* IVP Bible Dictionary Series. Downers Grove: IVP Academic, 2012.

Boring, Eugene M. "Early Christian Prophecy." In *ABD*, 5:495–502.

Briggs, Richard S. "Hermeneutics." In *DOP*, 318–33.

Brown, Jeannine K. "Jesus Messiah as Isaiah's Servant of the Lord: New Testament Explorations." *Journal of the Evangelical Theological Society* 63 (2020) 51–69.

Browning, Don S. *A Fundamental Practical Theology: Descriptive and Strategic Proposals.* Minneapolis: Fortress, 1991.

Brueggemann, Walter. "The Book of Jeremiah: Portrait of the Prophet." *Interpretation* 37 (1983) 130–45.

———. *A Commentary on Jeremiah: Exile and Homecoming.* Grand Rapids: Eerdmans, 1998.

———. *Mandate to Difference: An Invitation to the Contemporary Church.* Louisville: Westminster John Knox, 2007.

———. *The Practice of the Prophetic Imagination: Preaching an Emancipating Word.* Minneapolis: Fortress, 2012.

———. *The Prophetic Imagination.* 40th anniv. ed. Minneapolis: Fortress, 2018.

———. *Theology of the Old Testament: Testimony, Dispute, Advocacy.* Minneapolis: Fortress, 1997.

Buber, Martin. *The Prophetic Faith.* Princeton: Princeton University Press, 2016.

Burgess, Stanley M., and Eduard M. van der Maas, eds. *The New International Dictionary of Pentecostal and Charismatic Movements.* Rev. ed. Grand Rapids: Zondervan, 2002.

Candy, Linda. "Practice Based Research: A Guide." CSS Report, November 2006. http://www.creativityandcognition.com/resources/PBR%20Guide-1.1-2006.pdf.

Cartledge, Mark J. "Charismatic Prophecy." *Journal of Empirical Theology* 8 (1995) 71–88.

———. "Charismatic Prophecy: A Definition and Description." *Journal of Pentecostal Theology* 5 (1994) 79–120.

———. "Charismatic Prophecy and New Testament Prophecy." *Themelios* 17 (1991) 17–19.

———. "Locating the Spirit in Meaningful Experience: Empirical Theology and Pentecostal Hermeneutics." In *Constructive Pneumatological Hermeneutics in Pentecostal Christianity*, edited by Kenneth J. Archer and L. William Oliverio Jr., 251–66. New York: Palgrave MacMillan, 2016.

———. *The Mediation of the Spirit: Interventions in Practical Theology.* Grand Rapids: Eerdmans, 2015.

———. *Narratives and Numbers: Empirical Studies of Pentecostal and Charismatic Christianity.* Global Pentecostal and Charismatic Studies 24. Leiden: Brill, 2017.

———. *Practical Theology: Charismatic and Empirical Perspectives.* Eugene, OR: Wipf & Stock, 2003.

Charette, Blaine. "'And Now for Something Completely Different': A 'Pythonic' Reading of Pentecost?" *Pneuma* 33 (2011) 59–62.

Childs, Brevard S. "The Canonical Shape of the Prophetic Literature." *Interpretation* 32 (1978) 45–55.

———. *Introduction to the Old Testament as Scripture.* Philadelphia: Fortress, 1979.

Compton, Bruce. "The Continuation of New Testament Prophecy and a Closed Canon: Revisiting Wayne Grudem's Two Levels of NT Prophecy." *Detroit Baptist Seminary Journal* 22 (2017) 57–73.

Cook, L. Stephen. *On the Question of the "Cessation of Prophecy" in Ancient Judaism.* Tübingen: Mohr Siebeck, 2011.

Cox, Harvey. *Fire from Heaven: The Rise of Pentecostal Spirituality and the Reshaping of Religion in the Twenty-First Century.* Cambridge, MA: Da Capo, 1995.

Creswell, John W., and Cheryl N. Poth. *Qualitative Inquiry and Research Design: Choosing among Five Approaches.* 4th ed. Thousand Oaks, CA: Sage, 2017.

Croatto, J. Severino. "Jesus, Prophet like Elijah, and Prophet-Teacher like Moses." *Journal of Biblical Literature* 124 (2005) 241–65.

Cross, Frank Moore. *Canaanite Myth and Hebrew Epic: Essays in the History of the Religion of Israel.* Cambridge: Harvard University Press, 1997.

Crouter, Richard. "Shaping an Academic Discipline: The *Brief Outline on the Study of Theology.*" In *The Cambridge Companion to Friedrich Schleiermacher,* edited by Jacqueline Mariña, 111–28. New York: Cambridge University Press, 2005.

Davies, Andrew. "Jeremiah." In *A Biblical Theology of the Holy Spirit,* edited by Trevor J. Burke and Keith Warrington, 46–56. London: SPCK, 2014.

Dayton, Donald W. *Theological Roots of Pentecostalism.* Grand Rapids: Baker Academic, 1987.

Dearman, J. Andrew. "Jeremiah: History of Interpretation." In *DOP,* 441–49.

Dubovský, Peter. "From Miracle-Makers Elijah and Elisha to Jesus and Apocrypha." *Studia Biblica Slovaca* 12 (2020) 24–42.

Farley, Edward. "Interpreting Situations: An Inquiry into the Nature of Practical Theology." In *Formation and Reflection: The Promise of Practical Theology,* edited by Lewis S. Mudge and James N. Poling, 1–25. Minneapolis: Fortress, 2009.

Farnell, F. David. "Fallible New Testament Prophecy/Prophets? A Critique of Wayne Grudem's Hypothesis." *Master's Seminary Journal* 2 (1991) 157–79.

Faupel, D. William. "The New Order of the Latter Rain: Restoration or Renewal?" In *Winds from the North: Canadian Contributions to the Pentecostal Movement,* edited by Michael Wilkinson and Peter Althouse, 239–63. Leiden: Brill, 2010.

Fee, Gordon D. *The First Epistle to the Corinthians.* Grand Rapids: Eerdmans, 1987.

———. "Gifts of the Spirit." In *Dictionary of Paul and His Letters,* edited by Gerald F. Hawthorne, Ralph P. Martin, and Daniel G. Reid, 339–47. Downers Grove: InterVarsity, 1993.

Fergusson, Neil. "Practice-Led Theology or Thinking Theology through Practice." PhD diss., University of Notre Dame, Fremantle, Australia, 2014.

Freedman, David Noel, ed. *The Anchor Bible Dictionary.* 6 vols. New York: Doubleday, 1992.

Fretheim, Terence E. *The Suffering of God: An Old Testament Perspective.* Minneapolis: Fortress, 1984.

Friebel, Kelvin G. *Jeremiah's and Ezekiel's Sign-Acts: Rhetorical Nonverbal Communication.* Sheffield, UK: Sheffield Academic, 1999.

———. "Sign Acts." In *DOP,* 707–13.

Gallagher, Shaun. *Phenomenology.* New York: Palgrave MacMillan, 2012.

Gee, Donald. *Concerning Spiritual Gifts.* Rev. ed. Springfield: Gospel, 1980.

Glazov, G. Y. "Canonical Criticism." In *DOP,* 77–83.

Glock, Charles Y., and Rodney Stark. *Religion and Society in Tension.* Chicago: Rand McNally, 1965.

Graham, Elaine. *Transforming Practice: Pastoral Theology in an Age of Uncertainty.* Eugene, OR: Wipf & Stock, 1996.

Gray, Carole. "Inquiry through Practice: Developing Appropriate Research Strategies." In *No Guru, No Method? Conference Proceedings,* edited by P. Korvenmaa. Research Institute, University of Art and Design, 1996. http://carolegray.net/Papers%20PDFs/ngnm.pdf.

Green, Chris E. W. "Beautifying the Beautiful Word: Scripture, the Triune God, and the Aesthetics of Interpretation." In *Constructive Pneumatological Hermeneutics in Pentecostal Christianity*, edited by Kenneth J. Archer and L. William Oliverio Jr., 103–19. New York: Palgrave MacMillan, 2016.

Green, Joel B. *The Gospel of Luke*. New International Commentary on the New Testament. Grand Rapids: Eerdmans, 1997.

Greenspan, Frederick. "Why Prophecy Ceased." *Journal of Biblical Literature* 108 (1989) 37–49.

Grey, Jacqueline. "Reading Isaiah 6 as a Testimony of Religious Experience." *Journal of Youngsan Theology* 53 (2020) 77–107. https://doi.org/10.18804/jyt.2020.09.53.77.

Grudem, Wayne. *The Gift of Prophecy in 1 Corinthians*. Lanham, MD: University Press of America, 1982.

———. *The Gift of Prophecy in the New Testament and Today*. Rev. ed. Wheaton, IL: Crossway, 2000.

———. "Why Christians Can Still Prophesy." *Christianity Today* 32 (1988) 29–35.

Harris, Tania. "Hearing God's Voice: Towards a Theology of Pentecostal Revelatory Experience." PhD diss., Alphacrucis College, Parramatta, Australia, 2020.

———. "The Wacky, the Frightening and the Spectacular: Hearing God's Voice in Australian Pentecostal Churches." In *Australian Pentecostal and Charismatic Movements: Arguments from the Margins*, edited by Christina Rocha, Mark P. Hutchinson, and Kathleen Openshaw, 194–213. Leiden: Brill, 2020.

———. "Where Pentecostalism and Evangelicalism Part Ways: Towards a Theology of Pentecostal Revelatory Experience Part 1." *Asian Journal of Pentecostal Studies* 23 (2020) 31–40.

———. "Where Pentecostalism and Evangelicalism Part Ways: Towards a Theology of Pentecostal Revelatory Experience Part 2." *Asian Journal of Pentecostal Studies* 23 (2020) 41–56.

Heidegger, Martin. *The Basic Problems of Phenomenology*. Bloomington: Indiana University Press, 1988.

———. *Being and Time*. Albany: State University of New York Press, 2010.

Heroin, Gary A. "Wrath of God (OT)." In *ABD*, 6:989–96.

Heschel, Abraham J. *The Prophets*. New York: Perennial Classics, 2001.

Hinck, Joel. "Heavenly Harmony: An Audio Analysis of Corporate Singing in Tongues." *Pneuma* 40 (2018) 167–91.

Holladay, William Lee. "Background of Jeremiah's Self-Understanding: Moses, Samuel, and Psalm 22." *Journal of Biblical Literature* 83 (1964) 153–64.

———. "Elusive Deuteronomists, Jeremiah, and Proto-Deuteronomy." *Catholic Biblical Quarterly* 66 (2004) 55–77.

———. *Jeremiah 1: A Commentary on the Book of the Prophet Jeremiah (Chapters 1–25)*. Hermeneia. Minneapolis: Fortress, 1986.

Hollenweger, Walter J. *Pentecostalism: Origins and Developments Worldwide*. Grand Rapids: Baker Academic, 1997.

———. *The Pentecostals*. London: SCM, 1972.

Huddleston, Jonathan. "What Would Elijah and Elisha Do? Internarrativity in Luke's Story of Jesus." *Journal of Theological Interpretation* 5 (2001) 265–82.

Husserl, Edmund. *The Idea of Phenomenology*. The Hague: Martinus Nijhoff, 1973.

———. *On the Phenomenology of the Consciousness of Internal Time (1893–1917)*. Translated by J. B. Brough. Dordrecht: Kluwer Academic, 1991.

Jenni, Ernst, and Claus Westermann, eds. *Theological Lexicon of the Old Testament.* Translated by Mark Biddle. 3 vols. Peabody, MA: Hendrickson, 1997.

Josephus. *Jewish Antiquities, Books I–IV.* Translated by H. St. J. Thackeray. 9 vols. Loeb Classical Library. Cambridge: Harvard University Press, 1961.

Keener, Craig S. *Acts: An Exegetical Commentary.* 4 vols. Grand Rapids: Baker Academic, 2012.

———. *Spirit Hermeneutics: Reading Scripture in Light of Pentecost.* Grand Rapids: Eerdmans, 2016.

Lamb, David T. "Word of God." In *DOP*, 860–67.

Land, Steven Jack. *Pentecostal Spirituality: A Passion for the Kingdom.* Cleveland: CPT, 2010.

LeVasseur, Jeanne J. "The Problem of Bracketing in Phenomenology." *Qualitative Health Research* 13 (2003) 408–420.

Levenson, Jon D. "Some Unnoticed Connotations in Jeremiah 20:9." *Catholic Biblical Quarterly* 46 (1984) 223–25.

Levison, John R. *Filled with the Spirit.* Grand Rapids: Eerdmans, 2009.

Lum, Dennis. *The Practice of Prophecy: An Empirical-Theological Study of Pentecostals in Singapore.* Eugene, OR: Pickwick, 2018.

Lundbom, Jack R. "Baruch." In *ABD*, 1:617.

———. "Jeremiah." In *ABD*, 3:684–98.

———. *Jeremiah Closer Up: The Prophet and the Book.* Sheffield, UK: Sheffield Phoenix, 2010.

———. *Jeremiah: Prophet Like Moses.* Eugene, OR: Cascade, 2015.

———. "Prophets in the Hebrew Bible." Oxford Research Encyclopedia of Religion, May 2016. https://doi.org/10.1093/acrefore/9780199340378.013.109.

Manen, Max van. *Phenomenology of Practice: Meaning-Giving Methods in Phenomenological Research and Writing.* New York: Routledge, 2014.

Matthews, Victor H. *The Hebrew Prophets and Their Social World: An Introduction.* 2nd ed. Grand Rapids: Baker Academic, 2012. Kindle edition.

McGuire, Meredith B. "The Social Context of Prophecy: 'Word-Gifts' of the Spirit among Catholic Pentecostals." *Review of Religious Research* 18 (1977) 134–47.

McMaster Divinity College. "Doctor of Practical Theology." https://mcmasterdivinity.ca/programs/doctor-practical-theology.

McQueen, Larry R. *Joel and the Spirit: The Cry of a Prophetic Hermeneutic.* Cleveland: CPT, 2009.

Menzies, Robert P. *The Development of Early Christian Pneumatology with Special Reference to Luke-Acts.* Sheffield, UK: Sheffield Academic, 1991.

Merleau-Ponty, Maurice. *Phenomenology of Perception.* New York: Routledge, 2013.

Michaels, J. Ramsey. "Gifts of the Spirit." In *NIDPCM*, 664–67.

Miller, Patrick D. "Book of Jeremiah." In *New Interpreter's Bible*, edited by Leander E. Keck et al., 6:554–926. Nashville: Abingdon, 2001.

Miller, Thomas William. *Canadian Pentecostals: A History of the Pentecostal Assemblies of Canada.* Mississauga, ON: Full Gospel, 1994.

Mittelstadt, Martin, and Caleb Howard Courtney. *Canadian Pentecostal Reader: The First Generation of Pentecostal Voices in Canada (1907–1925).* Cleveland: CPT, 2021.

Moore, Rickie D. *The Spirit of the Old Testament.* Journal of Pentecostal Theology Supplement Series 35. Leiden: Brill, 2011.

Moustakas, Clark. *Phenomenological Research Methods.* Thousand Oaks, CA: Sage, 1994.

Moyise, Steve. "Prophets in the New Testament." In *DOP*, 650–57.

Mudge, Lewis S., and James N. Poling, eds. *Formation and Reflection: The Promise of Practical Theology*. Minneapolis: Fortress, 2009.

Muindi, Samuel W. "The Nature and Significance of Prophecy in Pentecostal-Charismatic Experience: An Empirical-Biblical Study." PhD diss., University of Birmingham, 2012.

———. *Pentecostal-Charismatic Prophecy: Empirical-Theological Analysis*. Oxford: Lang, 2017.

Noel, Bradley Truman. *Pentecostal and Postmodern Hermeneutics: Comparisons and Contemporary Impact*. Eugene, OR: Wipf & Stock, 2010.

Osmer, Richard R. *Practical Theology: An Introduction*. Grand Rapids: Eerdmans, 2008.

Oswalt, John N. *The Book of Isaiah: Chapters 1–39*. New International Commentary on the Old Testament. Grand Rapids: Eerdmans, 1986.

Overholt, Thomas W. "The End of Prophecy: No Players without a Program." *Journal for the Study of the Old Testament* 42 (1988) 103–15.

———. "Jeremiah 27–29: The Question of False Prophecy." *Journal of the American Academy of Religion* 35 (1967) 241–49.

PAOC. "Contemporary Prophets and Prophecy." Position paper. November 2007. https://www.paoc.org/docs/default-source/church-toolbox/position-papers/contemporary-prophets-prophecy/contemporary-prophets-and-prophecy.pdf.

———. "PAOC Statement of Affirmation Regarding the Equality of Women and Men in Leadership." June 2018. https://www.paoc.org/docs/default-source/church-toolbox/position-papers/statements/paoc-statement-of-affirmation-regarding-the-equality-of-women-and-men-in-leadership.pdf.

———. "Statement of Essential Truths." May 2022. https://paoc.org/docs/default-source/fellowship-services-documents/constitutions/2022/statement-of-essential-truths-2022.pdf.

———. "Statement of Fundamental and Essential Truths." 2014. https://www.paoc.org/docs/default-source/fellowship-services-documents/statement-of-fundamental-and-essential-truths.pdf.

Pattison, Stephen, and James Woodward. "An Introduction to Pastoral and Practical Theology." In *The Blackwell Reader in Pastoral and Practical Theology*, 1–19. Malden: Blackwell, 2000.

Patton, John H. *From Ministry to Theology: Pastoral Action and Reflection*. Eugene, OR: Wipf & Stock, 1995.

Phinney, D. Nathan. "Call/Commission Narratives." In *DOP*, 65–71.

Polk, Timothy. *The Prophetic Persona: Jeremiah and the Language of the Self*. Sheffield, UK: JSOT, 1984.

Poloma, Margaret M. *Main Street Mystics: The Toronto Blessing and Reviving Pentecostalism*. Walnut Creek,CA: AltaMira, 2003.

Reed, David A. "Oneness Pentecostalism." In *NIDPCM*, 936–44.

Riss, Richard M. "Latter Rain Movement." In *NIDPCM*, 830–33.

Robeck, Cecil M., Jr. "A Pentecostal Perspective on Prophetic Gifts." *Asian Journal of Pentecostal Studies* 23 (2020) 108–37.

———. "Prophecy, Gift of." In *NIDPCM*, 999–1012.

Roberts, Kyle. "Jon Stewart: A Prophetic Satirist or Satirical Prophet?" *Unsystematic Theology with Kyle Roberts*, August 6, 2015. http://www.patheos.com/blogs/

unsystematictheology/2015/08/jon-stewart-a-prophetic-satirist-or-satirical-prophet.

Rosenberg, Joel. "Jeremiah and Ezekiel." In *The Literary Guide to the Bible*, edited by Robert Alter and Frank Kermode, 184–206. Cambridge, MA: Belknap, 1987.

Rossi, Benedetta. "Reshaping Jeremiah: Scribal Strategies and the Prophet Like Moses." *Journal for the Study of the Old Testament* 44 (2020) 575–93.

Runck, Jared Scott. "A Pentecostal 'Hearing' of the Confessions of Jeremiah: The Literary Figure of the Prophet Jeremiah as an Ideal Hearer of the Word." DTh diss., University of South Africa, 2017.

Samuel, Josh P. S. *The Holy Spirit in Worship Music, Preaching, and the Altar: Renewing Pentecostal Corporate Worship*. Cleveland: CPT, 2018.

Sanders, James A. *From Sacred Story to Sacred Text: Canon as Paradigm*. Philadelphia: Fortress, 1987.

Sartre, Jean-Paul. *Being and Nothingness*. New York: Washington Square, 1993.

Schlimm, Matthew R. "Different Perspectives on Divine Pathos: An Examination of Hermeneutics in Biblical Theology." *Catholic Biblical Quarterly* 69 (2007) 673–94.

Schmitt, John J. "Preexilic Hebrew Prophecy." In *ABD*, 5:482–89.

Seitz, Christopher R. "The Prophet Moses and the Canonical Shape of Jeremiah." *Zeitschrift für die alttestamentliche Wissenschaft* 101 (1989) 3–27.

Selms, Adrianus van. "Telescoped Discussion as a Literary Device in Jeremiah." *Vetus Testamentum* 26 (1976) 99–112.

Seymour, William. *The Azusa Papers*. Monee, IL: Dream, 2014.

Shead, Andrew G. *A Mouth Full of Fire*. Downers Grove: InterVarsity, 2012.

Smith, Mark S. *The Laments of Jeremiah and Their Contexts*. Atlanta: Scholars, 1990.

Sommer, Benjamin D. "Did Prophecy Cease? Evaluating a Reevaluation." *JBL* 115 (1995) 31–47.

Spittler, Russell P. "Glossolalia." In *NIDPCM*, 670–76. Grand Rapids: Zondervan, 2002.

Stewart, Adam, and Andrew Gabriel. "Highlights from the 2014 Survey of PAOC Credential Holders: Including Key Comparisons with Carl Verge's 1985/86 Survey." http://paocbeliefs.weebly.com/uploads/3/7/3/4/37340129/highlights_from_the_2014_survey_of_paoc_credential_holders_22-01-2015.pdf.

———. "Missional Vitality and the Future of the PAOC." *Enrich: The Leadership Magazine of the Pentecostal Assemblies of Canada* (Fall 2015) 22–25.

———. "Spiritual Vitality among PAOC Credential Holders." *Enrich: The Leadership Magazine of the Pentecostal Assemblies of Canada* (Summer 2015) 26–29.

———. "Theological Vitality in the PAOC Today." *Enrich: The Leadership Magazine of the Pentecostal Assemblies of Canada* (Spring 2015) 12–15.

Stewart, Adam, et al. "Changes in Clergy Belief and Practice in Canada's Largest Pentecostal Denomination." *Pneuma* 39 (2017) 145–81.

Stokl, Jonathan. "Ancient Near Eastern Prophecy." In *DOP*, 16–24.

Stone, Michael E., and Matthias Henze. *4 Ezra and 2 Baruch: Translations, Introductions, and Notes*. Minneapolis: Fortress, 2013,

Strabo. *Geography: Books 8–9*. Translated by Horace Leonard Jones. Loeb Classical Library. Cambridge: Harvard University Press, 2001.

Strawn, Brent A., and Brad D. Strawn. "Prophecy and Psychology." In *DOP*, 610–23.

Stronstad, Roger. *The Charismatic Theology of St. Luke: Trajectories from the Old Testament to Luke-Acts*. 2nd ed. Grand Rapids: Baker, 2012.

————. *The Prophethood of All Believers: A Study in Luke's Charismatic Theology.* Cleveland: CPT, 1999.

————. "Review of John R. Levison's *Filled with the Spirit* Part III, Early Christian Literature Chapter 3, 'Filled with the Spirit and the Book of Acts.'" *Journal of Pentecostal Theology* 20 (2011) 201–206.

————. *Spirit Scripture and Theology: A Pentecostal Perspective.* 2nd ed. Baguio, Philippines: Asia Pacific Theological Seminary Press, 2018.

Swinton, John, and Harriet Mowat. *Practical Theology and Qualitative Research.* 2nd ed. London: SCM, 2016.

Tappeiner, Daniel A. "A Psychological Paradigm for the Interpretation of the Charismatic Phenomenon of Prophecy." *Journal of Psychology and Theology* 5 (1977) 23–29.

Thiselton, Anthony C. "The Supposed Power of Words in the Biblical Writings." *Journal of Theological Studies* 25 (1974) 283–99.

Thomas, Brynmor. "The Teaching and Practice of the Apostolic Church, with Special Reference to Its Concept of Directive Prophecy." PhM diss., Bangor University, Wales, 2016.

Thompson, J. A. *The Book of Jeremiah.* New International Commentary on the Old Testament. Grand Rapids: Eerdmans, 1980.

Tiemeyer, Lena-Sofia. "Ezekiel: Book of." In *DOP*, 214–19.

Todres, Les. *Embodied Enquiry: Phenomenological Touchstones for Research, Psychotherapy and Spirituality.* New York: Palgrave MacMillan, 2007.

Torwalt, Bryan, and Katie Torwalt. "Holy Spirit." Capitol CMG Genesis and Jesus Culture Music, 2011.

Turner, Max. *The Holy Spirit and Spiritual Gifts.* Grand Rapids: Baker Academic, 1996.

————. "Spiritual Gifts Then and Now." *Vox Evangelica* 15 (1985) 7–63.

Urbach, Ephraim. "When Did Prophecy Cease?" *Tarbiz* 17 (1946) 1–11.

Vondey, Wolfgang. *Pentecostal Theology: Living the Full Gospel.* New York: T. & T. Clark, 2018.

Vondey, Wolfgang, and Chris W. Green. "Between This and That: Reality and Sacramentality in the Pentecostal Worldview." *Journal of Pentecostal Theology* 19 (2010) 243–64.

Wessels, Wilhelm J. "'My Word Is Like Fire': The Consuming Power of YHWH's Word." *Old Testament Essays* 24 (2011) 492–510.

————. "Prophet versus Prophet in the Book of Jeremiah: In Search of the True Prophets." *Old Testament Essays* 22 (2009) 733–51.

————. "Prophetic Sensing of Yahweh's Word." *HTS Teologiese Studies/Theological Studies* 71 (2015) 1–9. https://doi.org/10.4102/hts.v71i3.2923.

Wadholm, Rick, Jr. *A Theology of the Spirit in the Former Prophets: A Pentecostal Perspective.* Cleveland: CPT, 2018.

Wertz, Marcia Stanley, et al. "The Composite First Person Narrative: Texture, Structure, and Meaning in Writing Phenomenological Descriptions." *International Journal of Qualitative Studies in Health and Well-Being* 6 (2011). https://doi.org/10.3402/qhw.v6i2.5882.

White, Ellen G. *Yahweh's Council: Its Structure and Membership.* Tübingen: Mohr Siebeck, 2014.

Wilkinson, Michael, and Peter Althouse. *Catch the Fire: Soaking Prayer and Charismatic Renewal.* DeKalb: Northern Illinois University Press, 2014.

———. "Like a Mighty Rushing Wind: Innovation and the Transnational Character of Pentecostalism." In *Winds from the North: Canadian Contributions to the Pentecostal Movement*, edited by Michael Wilkinson and Peter Althouse, 1–13. Leiden: Brill, 2010.

Wilson, Robert R. "Prophecy and Ecstasy: A Reexamination." *Journal of Biblical Literature* 98 (1979) 321–37.

Wolff, Hans Walter. *Hosea: A Commentary on the Book of the Prophet Hosea*. Hermeneia. Minneapolis: Fortress, 1988.

Woodward, James, and Stephen Pattison, eds. *The Blackwell Reader in Pastoral and Practical Theology*. Malden, MA: Blackwell, 2000.

Yong, Amos. "The Science, Sighs, and Signs of Interpretation: An Asian American Post-Pentecostal Hermeneutics in a Multi-, Inter-, and Trans-cultural World." In *Constructive Pneumatological Hermeneutics in Pentecostal Christianity*, edited by Kenneth J. Archer and L. William Oliverio Jr., 177–95. New York: Palgrave MacMillan, 2016.

———. *Spirit-Word-Community: Theological Hermeneutics in Trinitarian Perspective*. Eugene, OR: Wipf & Stock, 2002.